CAPE TOWN

BY
MIKE CADMAN

Produced by
Thomas Cook Publishing

King Protea

Written by Mike Cadman

Original photography by Mike Cadman and Trevor Samson

Original design by Laburnum Technologies PVT Ltd

Cover design by Liz Lyon Design, Oxford

Editing and page layout by Jacana Media

Published by Thomas Cook Publishing
A division of Thomas Cook Tour
Operations Limited

PO Box 227, The Thomas Cook Business Park, Units 15–16, Coningsby Road, Peterborough PE3 8SB, United Kingdom

E-mail: books@thomascook.com

www.thomascookpublishing.com

ISBN: 1-841574-30-9

Text © 2005 Thomas Cook Publishing

Maps © 2005 Thomas Cook Publishing

First edition © 2005 Thomas Cook Publishing

Head of Thomas Cook Publishing: Chris Young

Project Editor: Charlotte Christensen

Project Administrator: Michelle Warrington

Production/DTP: Steven Collins

Printed and bound in Spain by: Grafo Industrias Gráficas, Basauri

Front cover credits: left © Peter Titmuss/Alamy; centre © Yadid Levy/Alamy; right © Walter Bibikow/Getty Images. Back cover credits: left © Paul Souders/Getty Images; right © Walter Bibikow/Getty Images.

Title page: Cape Town coastline (South African Tourism)

C o n t e n t s

Store in Bo Kaap

Introduction

Cape Town is a beautiful city, and the grandeur of the Cape Peninsula has impressed people for centuries. Many South Africans call it 'The Mother City', others 'The Tavern of the Seas'. Perhaps Sir Francis Drake had it right when in the 16th century, after rounding the Cape, he described the region as 'the fairest Cape we saw in the whole circumference of the Earth'.

Protea – South Africa's national flower

Today millions of people from around the world seem to agree with Drake's description, because Cape Town and its surrounding areas are the country's top tourist attractions. Sheltering in the shadow of its trademark, Table Mountain, Cape Town is a city of beaches and hiking trails, vibrant nightlife and good food and wine.

It is also a city, along with all of South Africa, that has a turbulent political history of racial discrimination and prejudice. The contrast between

Cape Town as millions of people have seen the city from Table Mountain

rich and poor is there for all to see, and a visit to the dusty Cape Flats reveals sprawling shantytowns where people live in poverty, a legacy of apartheid. Under apartheid many people were forced to live on the Flats, and were not allowed to move elsewhere because of their race.

But whether Capetonians live in the mansions of Bishopscourt or the small square houses of Bonteheuwel, they pride themselves on knowing how to have fun and to enjoy the scenic splendour that surrounds them.

On weekends and during holidays, the beaches, mountain walks and picnic sites attract families out for a day in the fresh air, while the more energetic ride bikes, jog, surf and even jump off the high peaks with hang-gliders and parasails. Some head to the nearby winelands to eat and enjoy delicious wines, while others visit the pretty valleys merely to enjoy the spectacular scenery. Back in the city the bars and clubs of Long Street, Camps Bay, De Waterkant and the V & A Waterfront fill up in the evenings as people settle down to continue their pursuit of enjoyment.

Cape Town is the oldest city in the country, and some buildings, many of which have been restored, date back to the 17th century. Mosques, synagogues and churches attest to the many cultures that mix in the city as do the variety of artistic styles and culinary preferences.

The city was founded in 1652 when the Dutch landed in what is today Cape Town, and established a post to replenish their ships. They soon came in contact with the Khoikhoi, a group of people who were primarily herders, and San hunter-gatherers who had been passing through the region for thousands of years making use of the region's natural resources.

Both the Indian and Atlantic oceans fringe the Cape coastline. Ranges of high fold-mountains roll across the landscape, and in the east thick indigenous forests provide a contrast to the semi-deserts of the Karoo, which forms the northern boundary of the province.

The *fynbos* vegetation which dominates the region is the richest floral kingdom in the world, hosting more than 7,300 species, 65 per cent of which occur nowhere else on the planet. The coast also offers some of the world's best sightings of southern right whales and their newborn calves.

Smaller towns in the winelands and further inland have followed Cape Town's lead and have created healthy tourism industries based on the wine farms, mountains and good scenery. They are as much a part of Cape Town's attractions as the city itself.

Fynbos vegetation dominates the Western Cape region

Geography and Climate

The Western Cape generally has a comfortable climate that is seldom extreme. Yes, sometimes very strong gales and winter storms blow in from the surrounding oceans, and in summer some days can be very hot, but the weather is usually fairly benign. Cape Town is the southernmost city in the vast expanse of Africa, lying some 11,840km (18,940 miles) away from its northern counterpart of Tunis, the capital of Tunisia. And, like Tunis, Cape Town has a Mediterranean climate with warm to hot summers and cool, wet winters.

Rugged Cape Point

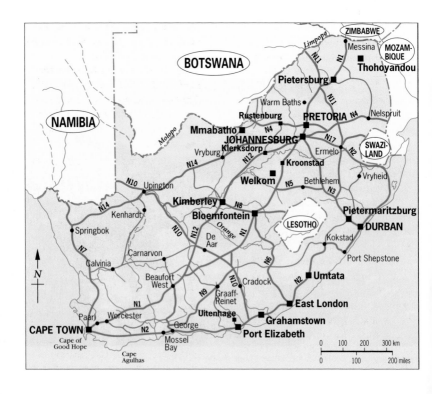

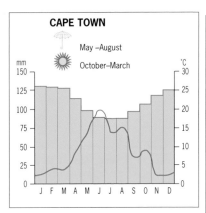

CAPE TOWN

May –August

October–March

mm	°C
150	30
125	25
100	20
75	15
50	10
25	5
0	0

J F M A M J J A S O N D

The warm, dry summer peaks between December and February, with daytime temperatures averaging at around 27–28°C (80–82°F) – although on some days the mercury reaches the mid-30s (±95°F). Winters are cool and wet, but temperatures seldom drop much lower than 8°C (16°F), and most of the rain falls in June and July. Snow sometimes falls on the nearby Hottentots Holland mountains and other peaks further inland.

Although winter days can be wet and gloomy, the weather often clears with a string of warm, clear days reminding everyone of summer.

Perhaps the most dramatic and best-known, and some would say notorious, element of Cape Town's weather is 'The Southeaster' – a powerful gale that sometimes blows the unwary or elderly off their feet. The wind, also known to locals as 'The Cape Doctor' because it brings clean air in from the oceans, causes clouds to form on the mountains, and is responsible for the 'tablecloth' that drapes itself over the flat top of Table Mountain.

Mountains are as much of an attraction of the Western Cape as are its beaches. Within a few hours drive of the city there are several ranges high enough to get winter snow. The Jonkershoek, Groot Drakenstein, Wemmershoek and Franschhoek mountains all tower over the winelands, their steep slopes and deep valleys creating microclimates that influence the flavour of wines made from the grapes grown there. Further afield the Hex River mountains and the Langeberg also influence local climates. There are countless hiking trails through these mountains, which offer a huge variety of other outdoor activities too.

The Karoo semi-deserts begin north of these fold mountains, and here temperatures often climb to 40°C (66°F) in summer, and in winter often plummet to well below 0°C (32°F).

To the north and northeast lies the rest of South Africa which covers some 1,2 million sq km, which is more than twice the size of France or a bit bigger than the US states of California and Texas combined.

Cape Town's trade mark, Table Mountain

It lies roughly from 22–35° south of the equator, and has 2,950km (1,833 miles) of coastline washed by the Atlantic Ocean in the west and Indian Ocean in the east.

South Africa shares borders with Namibia, Botswana, Zimbabwe, Mozambique, Swaziland and Lesotho – the latter is entirely surrounded by South Africa.

Flora and Fauna

Early naturalists reported both black rhino and lions occurring within sight of Table Mountain but, sadly, large game was shot out very quickly after the arrival of settlers with firearms. Elephants and buffalo also occurred in the Western Cape, but it unlikely that they were found in any great numbers, because the predominant plants are part of the *fynbos* which is low in nutrients and unsuitable for large numbers of big herbivores.

(*Fynbos* is a name derived from the Dutch word *fyn* relating to fine or narrow leaves and *bos*, meaning bush.)

Hippos occurred in small numbers, and some have been re-introduced to the Rondevlei Nature Reserve a few kilometres from the centre of the city. Small numbers of the endemic bontebok (they only occur naturally in the Western Cape), reedbuck, grysbok, klipspringer and other species are protected in the Table Mountain National Park at Good Hope Nature Reserve.

Many smaller mammals are quite common, and are found throughout the region. These include the porcupine (Africa's largest rodent), Cape clawless otters, yellow mongooses and the ubiquitous rock dassie, commonly misidentified as a rock rabbit. The dassie, or more correctly the rock hyrax, lives on rocky slopes and is the primary prey of the black eagle. Several pairs of these

Cape sugarbird among flowering pincushion proteas

Copyright: South African Tourism

large raptors, with wingspans of over 2m (6,6ft), nest close to Cape Town, and can sometimes be seen soaring near the Table Mountain Cableway or high above the Kirstenbosch National Botanical Gardens.

Other raptors, including the lanner falcon, black sparrow hawk and jackal buzzard, are relatively common. Brightly coloured lesser-collared sunbirds are common *fynbos* residents, as well as the spectacular orange-breasted sunbird and Cape sugarbird.

In winter, albatrosses, petrels and other birds that usually spend most of their lives at sea are sometimes driven towards the coast by storms, and can occasionally be spotted near Cape Point.

The Cape's *fynbos* is described by botanists as a Plant Kingdom, and although the smallest, it is the richest of the six Plant Kingdoms that cover the world's surface.

Fynbos is comprised of different plant species including the proteas, many of which grace flower arrangements on tables across the world, as well as restios and ericas. A variety of orchids, irises and gladioli also help make up the *fynbos*.

Housing estates, golf courses, industrial complexes and other developments are causing significant damage to the indigenous vegetation, and many species are threatened. Alien plants have also encroached on large areas, although there are many programmes to remove these plants.

The *fynbos* also supports a wide variety of tortoises including the highly endangered geometric tortoise and the speckled padloper, the world's smallest tortoise. The world's greatest diversity of tortoises, 12 species, occur in southern Africa.

BABOONS

Baboons occur throughout the Cape Peninsula, and are often seen at the roadside, or, unfortunately, begging in parking lots or raiding people's refuse bins. Their intelligence, strength and speed enable baboons to take advantage of humans, and they do so regularly. People are often directly at fault because they feed the animals which then, unsurprisingly, learn to associate people with food. They can become very threatening or even dangerous when demanding food. A large male baboon, which can weigh over 35kg (77lb), is extremely strong, and its incisors, which are as long as those of a lion, are fearsome weapons. As a last resort, conservation authorities shoot baboons that have become a threat to humans.

Copyright: South African Tourism

Mother baboon feeding baby

History of Cape Town and South Africa

The British Hotel, Simon's Town

100,000 BC	Archaeological evidence shows southern Africa is already inhabited by *Homo sapiens* who used stone tools and fire.
8,000 BC	San hunters inhabit parts of South Africa.
AD 1–1500	Iron-working spreads through central and southern Africa as Bantu people begin to move southwards and dominate the San and Khoikhoi peoples.
1488	Bartholomeu Dias rounds the Cape and reaches Mossel Bay.
1497	Vasco da Gama rounds the Cape and charts the sea route to India.
1652	Arrival of Jan van Riebeeck, first commander of the Dutch East India Company's Cape settlement.
1654–57	First slaves from Indonesia and Madagascar arrive in the Cape.
1666	Work begins on what today is The Castle and South Africa's oldest building. Work is completed in 1679.
1679	The governor of the Cape, Simon van der Stel, is granted a large stand of land which he develops into Groot Constantia, now the oldest wine estate in the country.
1688	French Huguenots arrive.
1779	First of nine settler-Xhosa frontier wars in the Eastern Cape.
1795	First British occupation of the Cape.
1802	The Cape is returned to the Dutch.

1806	Second British occupation of the Cape.
1820	Large group of British settlers arrive in the Grahamstown area.
mid-1830s	The Great Trek into the interior begins as Boers grow resentful of British rule in the Cape colony.
1838	Battle of Blood River: a small force of Voortrekkers defeats the Zulu.
1840	The Cape Town municipality is created. The population is about 20,000.
1850s	Independent Boer republics of Orange Free State and Transvaal are established.
1859	The first railway is constructed from Cape Town to Paarl and Stellenbosch.
1860	Construction of the docks in Table Bay begins.
1867	Discovery of diamonds near Kimberley – the diamond rush begins.
1879	Battles of Isandhlwana and Rorke's Drift.

THE SOUTH AFRICAN WAR

Following its success in the First Anglo-Boer War (1880), the Transvaal Republic regained independence from Britain. By then its gold was attracting droves of foreign prospectors. British imperialists instigated the Jameson Raid (1895), hoping to ignite an uprising followed by the installation of a British administration. Its failure and ensuing events led to the South African War (1899). President Kruger's commandos defeated the British at Talana Hill and routed them at Nicholson's Nek, but their siege of Ladysmith was disastrous, and cost them the war. By 1900, Pretoria had surrendered. A rural guerrilla war resulted in savage retribution: Boer women and children were imprisoned in the world's first concentration camps. The horror of these led ultimately to the Peace of Vereeniging (1902).

Art gallery in a National Monument House, Church Street, Tulbach

1880	First Anglo-Boer War (won by the Boers).
1886	Gold discovered. Johannesburg founded.
1896	The first electric trams in Cape Town begin running.
1899–1902	The South African War (formerly the Anglo-Boer War) – won by the British.
1905	Cape Town is declared the legislative capital of South Africa.
1910	Union of South Africa formed.
1912	The African National Congress is formed.
1913	The Natives Land Act reserves most land for the use of White people.
1948	Victory for the National Party in White elections.
1950	Increasingly harsh apartheid legislation introduced and tightened during the next few years.
1952	The ANC's defiance campaign begins.

Historic cottage near Cape Point

1958	Dr Hendrik Verwoerd becomes prime minister. Apartheid strictly enforced.
1960	Referendum among Whites approves South African independence from Britain. Sharpeville Massacre: demonstrators against the Pass Laws are fired on (69 killed, 180 injured). State bans ANC.
1961	South Africa leaves the Commonwealth and becomes a republic. The ANC begins its armed struggle.
1964	Rivonia Treason Trial: Nelson Mandela and seven other ANC members are sentenced to life imprisonment. He and other prisoners are sent to Robben Island, within sight of Cape Town.

| 1966 | Tens of thousands of Coloured people are forced out of District Six when the government declares it a 'Whites only' area. |

| 1966 | Verwoerd assassinated by parliamentary messenger. |

| 1967 | Professor Chris Barnard performs the world's first heart transplant. The shanty towns of Crossroads, KTC and others begin gaining a foothold on the Cape Flats. |

| 1975 | South Africa invades Angola. |

| 1976 | Police open fire on student protestors in Soweto on 16 June. The shootings lead to nationwide rioting, including in Cape Town and surrounding areas, resulting in hundreds of deaths. |

| 1977 | Mandatory UN arms embargo. Steve Biko dies in detention. |

| 1980 | The Greenmarket Square fleamarket in Cape Town begins slowly, but by the end of the decade, the area is declared a pedestrian precinct. |

Ox-wagon wheels

THE GREAT TREK

In 1835, two groups of Dutch-speaking Boers left the Cape for the unknown interior in the Great Trek. They felt that the colonial government had failed to provide protection against the Xhosa in the never-ending battle for land, while the abolition of slavery had robbed them of valued possessions. One group of Voortrekkers, led by Piet Retief, went into Zulu Natal where Dingane massacred their advance party. Revenge was the horrible battle of Blood River, followed by the establishment of the Republic of Natalia (1838), which Britain annexed. The Boers then trekked north, and in 1860, founded the South African Republic (ZAR).

The other party of Voortrekkers trekked beyond the Vaal and Orange rivers, and proclaimed the Orange Free State (1854).

Die Kruithuis (the Arsenal) in Stellenbosch was built in 1777

1983	A new constitution allows three separate houses in parliament – for Whites, Coloureds and Indians.
1984	The United Democratic Front is launched in Mitchell's Plain, Cape Town. This movement plays a pivotal role in political opposition to the apartheid state.
1985	ANC President Oliver Tambo, Rev. Jesse Jackson and Archbishop Huddleston head a 100,000-strong march through London demanding sanctions.
1985–86	Thousands of people are detained without trial and a State of Emergency is declared. Cape Town and surrounding areas are swept by sporadic political protests and violence until the end of the decade.
1988	Work begins on the Cape Town Waterfront.
1989	F W de Klerk becomes president succeeding P W Botha.
1990	Nelson Mandela released from prison. National Party government abandons apartheid, and begins negotiations to end it.

1992	Whites-only referendum leads to a 69 per cent vote to continue reforms.
1993	Nelson Mandela and President F W de Klerk share the Nobel Peace Prize.
1994	Democratic elections in April; ANC President Nelson Mandela elected president of South Africa. South Africa re-enters the Commonwealth.
1995	The Truth and Reconciliation Commission under Archbishop Desmond Tutu is appointed to hear evidence of apartheid atrocities. Rugby World Cup held in Cape Town, the largest sporting event held in the country in decades.
1999	The second democratic election is held, and Mandela steps down as president. The ANC wins and Thabo Mbeki becomes president.
2004	The third democratic election is held, and the ANC returns to power again. Mbeki remains president.

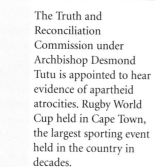

Political posters during the 2004 general election

THE LIBERATION STRUGGLE

Although it was formed in 1912, the ANC only resorted to taking up arms after it was banned by the state in 1960. Initially, most military actions took place in the form of sabotage of powerlines and other infrastructure, but in the 1970s and 80s armed guerrillas sometimes clashed with security forces and made bomb attacks against both strategic and civilian targets.

As the nationwide civil unrest of the 1980s intensified, ANC supporters also clashed with those of the Inkatha Freedom Party and others perceived to be supporters of the state. Troops and riot police patrolled the townships almost constantly from 1984, and clashed with ANC-supporting youths on a daily basis.

Governance

Cape Town today is a thriving city trying to deal with past injustices, and at the same time meet the challenges of the 21st century. Some plans work and some don't, but the majority of Capetonians are hard at work trying to create an economically viable city, free from the prejudices of the apartheid-era South Africa.

Parliament building

Cape Town has seen many changes of national government in its 350-year history, but none so significant as the election of Nelson Mandela as president after the country's first democratic election in 1994.

Mandela made his first public speech as a free man at the Grand Parade in Cape Town in 1990 before an ecstatic crowd, an event that everyone knew was pivotal to the future of South Africa and the city. This excitement was carried over into 1994, and the sheer relief that South Africa had achieved democracy without a full-scale war released a wave of euphoria still not forgotten.

Today everyone is allowed to vote for both national and regional representation in this once-divided city and country. In terms of the Constitution, everybody is treated equally by the state, and the country's laws should be applied fairly, irrespective of race or sex.

This equality was unthinkable in the last decades of the 20th century and, in fact, ever since the first colonists arrived.

A typically callous action took place in 1966 when the government decided that the Coloured people living in the lively District Six of Cape Town should be forcibly removed to live somewhere else. Bulldozers demolished the homes of tens of thousands of people who were loaded into trucks and forced to live on the dusty Cape Flats. The reason for the removal was simple: the people of District Six were not White, and the government decided they were living too close to the city.

A new generation of South Africans is growing up with no knowledge of apartheid

The South African Government has taken enormous strides towards improving housing conditions

The Cape Flats themselves were the scene of intense conflict, first in 1976 during the Soweto uprisings which had repercussions around the country, and later during the 1980s. One of the most notorious events of the time, the 'Trojan Horse Incident' took place in Athlone, a Coloured area, when policemen hidden in boxes on the back of a truck leapt out and opened fire with shotguns on stone-throwing children, killing three.

Cape Town's colonial history is a litany of possession and dispossession. When the first colonists arrived, they set about driving out local people or forcing them into labour. Many of the San and Khoikhoi people were wiped out by disease or killed in clashes with settlers.

As the colony began to spread its borders, settlers came in contact with the Xhosa and other tribes, and further clashes over cattle and land ensued.

The colony changed hands between the British and the Dutch in 1796, and again in 1806 when the British took over.

Later on in history, Dutch settlers upset at British rule and the abolition of slavery, packed their wagons in the 1830s and left for the interior, an event later known as The Great Trek. Cape Town was also a crucial port and railhead after the discovery of gold and diamonds, and during the South African War (formerly the Anglo-Boer War) of 1899–1902.

South African Politics

For much of the 1980s and early 1990s South Africa's political turmoil made international news headlines, and the name of Nelson Mandela became famous all over the world. South Africa's transition to democracy was hailed as an example of conciliation and common sense.

The country has now had three fully democratic elections, including the 1994 election, and although the ruling African National Congress (ANC) is by far the largest party, political debate and argument is vibrant and no more vituperative than in any other democracy. The ANC were returned to power in the 2004 election, and Thabo Mbeki was re-elected president for a second term.

After years of isolation, South Africa has become an important political and economic role-player in Africa, and the country's politicians have contributed significantly towards the slow process of establishing unity on a difficult continent.

South African diplomats have helped work towards the resolution of several wars in Africa, and have played an important role in trying to improve trade agreements, foreign debt write-offs, and other issues important to poor nations.

Although not all of the government's views, particularly with regard to the policies of some African countries' leaders and Middle Eastern politics, have met with the approval of developed nations, South Africa nevertheless maintains good relations with many countries around the globe.

Statue of Cecil John Rhodes in Cape Town

AIDS

The AIDS epidemic is one of the greatest issues facing South Africa, and has enormous social and economic consequences. Many children have been orphaned after their parents have died from AIDS-related diseases, and many skilled people are lost to the economy after falling sick and later dying. The government was initially very slow to respond to the crisis and, in many cases, the private sector took the lead in education and medication.

Nearly all AIDS in South Africa is spread through participating in unprotected sex. Blood transfusions in large hospitals are responsible for very few cases. Private hospitals use world-class technology.

Freedom of speech and the media is guaranteed by the constitution, as is the right to freedom of association – rights which were an anathema of the previous government of the country.

During the 1980s, the National Party (NP) Government clamped down hard on the popular uprising sweeping the Black townships, and tens of thousands of people, including children, were detained without trial. A series of States of Emergency were declared giving the police and military vast powers.

Thousands of people died in political conflict, many killed by police bullets. The political insurrection was the culmination of many events over the years.

Resistance against discrimination manifested itself in countless ways over the centuries, but it was only after the conservative National Party came to power in 1948 that parties such as the ANC began organised resistance in earnest.

By the mid-1980s, economic sanctions had tightened considerably, and this, coupled with the expense of fighting wars in neighbouring states, had a serious impact on the economy.

As the Berlin Wall was coming down, and many former Soviet States were undergoing their own liberation, the South African Government buckled under both internal and international pressure, and the government finally made the decision to release Mandela and un-ban political parties.

In 1990, Mandela walked free, and four years later, after prolonged and intense negotiations by representatives of nearly all South Africans, he ushered in a new South Africa to the salute of military helicopters flying the country's new flag and the acclaim of a rapturous nation.

The Independent Electoral Commission has run all three general elections since 1994, and ensures fairness and accountability among voters and officials alike

Culture

Many Capetonians portray their city as the cultural capital of South Africa and are proud of the large number of museums, art galleries and historical monuments that house some of the country's best exhibits and displays.

They are similarly proud of their theatre and musical traditions, and like to think of Cape Town as an important member of the world jazz community. Cape Town hosts two of the country's most important jazz festivals which attract artists from all over the world.

Painting displayed at a national art competition for the young

Art

The rock paintings and engravings of the San (Bushmen) pre-date the arrival of European settlers by thousands of years, and these valuable records of early life on the continent have become a much-treasured part of the country's cultural heritage (*see Box on opposite page*).

The first European artists were often explorers who recorded fantastic scenes with animals, which seemed to them, and their audiences, a strange and unexplored region.

In 1652 Dutchman Jodocus Hondius sent back drawings of all sorts of amazing creatures, including lions, rhinos and hippos, and this helped

Copyright: South African Tourism

San Rock paintings tell spiritual and other stories of daily life long ago

ART

Perhaps some of the most unusual art galleries in the country are the rock overhangs and shelters where San (Bushmen) artists used vegetable and animal-blood paints to record hunting, ceremonial and other scenes. The San wandered through South Africa as long as 40,000 years ago, and left one of the largest collections of rock art in the world scattered throughout the more mountainous areas of South Africa.

Their paintings and rock engravings tell stories of their daily life, but they also had spiritual significance. There are some paintings in the Western Cape, but the richest collections are found in the uKhahlamba-Drakensberg mountains in the Eastern Cape and KwaZulu-Natal.

African music shop in Long Street, Cape Town

spark interest among other explorers, scientists and artists.

Many of the more successful explorers were a combination of all three, and Robert Gordon (1743–95), Anders Sparrman (1748–1820) and Francois Levaillant (1753–1828) were prolific and accurate artists who carefully recorded the mammals, reptiles, birds, fish and insects they encountered.

Their records encouraged other artists, and the 18th and 19th centuries saw the development of a school of European artists intent on adding to the record of the landscapes, people and animals of this remarkable region.

Perhaps the best known of these painters were Thomas Baines and Thomas Bowler whose work created an accurate, if somewhat stylised, record of the country as it then was.

Black artists including George Pemba and Gerard Sekoto, although almost unknown in South Africa at the time, took this trend to a new level in the 1940s, and today their work fetches high prices. Later in the 20th century many artists began using their work as a form of protest against apartheid.

Modern South African art draws on many influences, and increasing numbers of young South Africans are focussing on more traditional African styles.

Music

Cape Town is the jazz capital of the country, and lovers of this form of music will be spoilt for choice among the many clubs and bars where jazz musicians strut their stuff. Abdullah Ibrahim formerly Dollar Brand *(see feature on p29)*, and Basil Coetzee, two of the icons of the Cape Town jazz

The Swellendam Dutch Reformed Church incorporates Gothic and Baroque architecture

Every year Cape Town hosts the North Sea Jazz Festival and the Jazzathon, which runs over four days.

But in Cape Town, as in the rest of South Africa, whether the music is played on a cowhide drum, a *marimba* (a form of xylophone usually made from a gourd), a Stradivarius violin or an electric guitar, someone will consider the entertainment 'traditional'. As with so many other aspects of the country, local music has its roots in many cultures and traditions, and is continually evolving according to new demands and trends.

In the 1980s, the Cape Town band, Bright Blue, cleverly interwove rock music, African rhythms and protest lyrics, and soon became one of the country's top groups. David Kramer, who was born in Worcester near Cape Town, manages to capture small-town South Africa in his music and singing, which is predominantly in Afrikaans, but is popular among English-speakers too.

Western and African influences mix easily, and radio stations and music stores offer everything from *kwaito* (a form of rap), reggae, jazz, blues, classical and hard rock to general pop.

Jazz trumpeter Hugh Masekela and singer Miriam Makeba have been known internationally since the 1960s, and younger artists such as Yvonne Chaka Chaka with her cross-cultural rhythms have built followings across Africa.

Johnny Clegg and his bands Juluka and Savuka pioneered a mix of traditional Zulu music and modern soft rock, while the Soweto String

community, learnt their music in the shadow of the mountain.

Ibrahim has achieved international fame, and has played all over the world including at the famous jazz festivals in Montreal, Berlin and Montreaux.

Coeztee, or 'Ou B' to insiders, rose to prominence after recording the classic 'Mannenberg' with Ibrahim in 1974. He later formed a band called Sebenza (which means 'work') and became a household name among jazz fans. He played with some of the country's top musicians, including Jonas Gwangwa and Hugh Masekela.

Quartet has managed to combine a mix of classical, jazz and African music into a huge popular product.

Architecture

Cape Town's architecture is a form of picture story-book that reflects the evolution of the city from open land in 1652 to the busy city it is today.

Cape Dutch, Edwardian, Art Deco, modern and simply plain-and-practical architecture all mixes easily in a city with a complex cultural background.

Perhaps the best-known form of South African architecture is the Cape Dutch style which is best displayed in Cape Town itself and the nearby wine making towns of Stellenbosch, Franschhoek, Paarl and Tulbagh where thatched-roof buildings with decorative gables and white walls preside over rows of vines. Most have large, ornate double doors and square windows with carefully tended wooden frames.

As Cape Town expanded, the authorities became concerned about the fire hazard posed by thatched roofs (a huge fire had swept through the town in 1736), and they encouraged the construction of houses with flat roofs,

Modern Cape Town is an important business hub

some of which can still be seen in the Bo Kaap area.

Many of the buildings that house Cape Town's museums were the work of some of the country's best-known architects and designers including Louis Thibault and, in later years, Sir Herbert Baker. Thibault designed parts of the Koopmans de Wet House and Rust en Vreugt among others. The prolific Baker designed the St George's Cathedral along Norman architectural lines, the Rhodes Building in Wale Street was influenced by his travels in Italy, and the Groote Schuur Estate is built in the Cape Dutch style. The massive Rhodes Memorial is a cross between Egyptian and Roman styles.

Perhaps the most easily recognised architectural landmark in the country are the Union Buildings in Pretoria built by Baker in 1912. The ornate buildings are decorated with stone pillars and friezes, and are still used as the seat of government.

Cape Town also has a good number of Victorian buildings which are also well represented in Durban, Pietermaritzburg and Oudtshoorn.

Elsewhere in South Africa, the older cities are a mix of glass and steel modernist structures, dull and conservative 1960s-office blocks and the occasional Art Deco or Victorian building. Residential architecture ranges from the opulent, built in whatever style

Cape Town is a mix of modern and pre-nineteenth century architecture, much of which has been restored

Copyright: South African Tourism

Youngsters get ready for a school play

the owner can afford, to the tiny almost square 'matchbox' houses built as housing for Black people in the formerly racially segregated townships.

In poor informal settlements, shacks are often made of corrugated iron sheeting, wooden crate panels and even plastic – they may not qualify as architectural masterpieces, but they are home to millions of people.

In rural areas, traditional Xhosa, Zulu or Venda huts are still used, but many have been adapted over the years. Zulu 'beehive' huts were made with grass thatched over a wooden frame, although traditional Xhosa and Venda homes tended to have mud walls.

Literature

Although most South African literature is written in English or Afrikaans, the country's writers have continually explored a wide range of themes and social issues, and their works largely trace the development of modern South Africa.

Many writers have achieved international recognition, and the Nobel Prize for Literature was awarded to two South Africans in recent years – Nadine Gordimer, (1991) and J M Coetzee (2003). Both writers, although very different in style, examine the psychology of apartheid and post-apartheid South Africa.

J M Coetzee was born in Cape Town, and his stark, desolate works explore the sense of despair many people felt during apartheid (*see feature on p28*).

The theme has been consistent among many writers, and the classic *Cry the Beloved Country* by Alan Paton (1948), *Down Second Avenue* by Es'kia Mphahlele (1959) and *Country of my Skull* by Antjie Krog (1998) dig deeply into the country's collective psyche.

South African poetry covers a very broad range of subjects from the South African War (Anglo-Boer War), through to a celebration of nature, love and the freedom struggle.

Poets, including Sipho Sepamala and Mafika Gwala, used their work to try to raise political awareness when other forms of political expression were outlawed.

South Africa has also produced many writers of popular fiction, and Wilbur Smith is one of the best-selling authors of all time. Although not literature in the classic sense, South Africa has a very strong publishing industry based on the environment and wildlife, and a huge variety of high-quality coffee table books, field guides and popular science works are available at good bookstores.

Drama

Capetonians often regard their city as the cultural centre of the country, and the 'Mother City' is suitably endowed with theatres, ranging from the formal to extremely casual and alternative venues.

The Baxter Theatre Centre and the Artscape Theatre Centre are the flagship venues with a long history of hosting everything from Shakespeare to Tom Stoppard and even opera. Some of the smaller theatres tend to be more

A performer delights tourists during a one-man show at the V & A Waterfront

experimental, but also manage to produce West End or Broadway favourites with aplomb.

Many South African playwrights and actors have achieved international fame, and Athol Fugard and John Kani have received critical acclaim in New York, London and elsewhere.

The performing arts have a strong base and long tradition in South Africa, and perhaps reached their peak in the last years of apartheid when theatre gave voice to protest that would otherwise have been silenced.

The Market Theatre complex in Johannesburg, and others, risked closure by running some political performances, and today that courage has been transformed into a desire to teach. Many theatres now run courses helping train aspiring actors.

Every year in June, Grahamstown in the Eastern Cape runs a week-long arts festival (*see Eastern Cape section on pp128–30*) where both established and fringe actors, playwrights and other performers strut their stuff. Various smaller festivals are hosted elsewhere in the country (*see Directory on pp30–1*).

South Africa's multi-cultural heritage is reflected in many forms of art and music

African Footprint, a big bold African musical, was a huge success, and even played to packed audiences in China.

Various symphony orchestras perform regularly, and some of the larger cities host ballets and opera, often with international guest artists performing.

A broad spectrum of people from across South Africa have made Cape Town their home

AFRICAN PEOPLE

Apart from the San (Bushmen) and the Khoikhoi (Hottentots), about 90 per cent of southern Africa's total population are Blacks whose ancestors migrated from the north. Some of these peoples dispersed into even more groups; the Nguni tribes (including Swazi, Xhosa and Zulu) eventually settled along the eastern seaboard, while the Sotho groups (Basotho, Pedi and Tswana) inhabited the South African plateau.

The Zulus went on to form themselves into strong kingdoms. Many migrant workers from neighbouring countries have, throughout this century, crossed South Africa's borders to man the gold and diamond mines.

J M Coetzee

JM Coetzee won the Nobel Prize for Literature in 2003, adding to an already illustrious literary career during which he became the first writer to win the Booker Prize twice.

Coetzees' writing is often stark and brutal, and in many of his works he delves into the harsh social and political realities of apartheid, and post-apartheid South Africa.

John Maxwell Coetzee was born in Cape Town on 9 February 1940, and spent most of his childhood there and in the farming town of Worcester on the edge of the Karoo.

His upbringing there is reflected in some of his writing when he describes the vast, lonely landscapes through which some of his characters travel. These desolate landscapes also are reflective of the political and social bleakness that Coetzee lived through.

He is an intensely private person, to the point of being reclusive. Coetzee graduated from the University of Cape Town in the early sixties, and worked in England before moving to the United States where he completed a doctorate in English Literature and Linguistics at the University of Texas. He also taught at the University of New York in Buffalo.

He was arrested during anti-Vietnam War protests and returned to South Africa. He retired as Professor of English from the University of Cape Town in 2002, and later moved to Australia.

He won the Booker Prize in 1983 for the *Life and Times of Michael K,* and again in 1999 with *Disgrace.* The only other South African to have won the Nobel Prize for literature is Nadine Gordimer who received the award in 1992.

Some of his other works include *Dusklands, In the Heart of the Country, Waiting for the Barbarians,* and *Foe and Elizabeth Costello: Eight Lessons.*

Below: JM Coetzee

AP Photo / Alastair Grant

Abdullah Ibrahim

Abdullah Ibrahim (Dollar Brand) is one of Cape Town's favourite sons, and his trademark jazz combined with African rhythms has influenced generations of young musicians. Although his parents called him Adolph Johannes Brand, he later adopted the name 'Dollar' although he finally dropped this name too. He was born in 1934, and began piano lessons at the age of seven. Ibrahim played with another South African great, the trumpet player Hugh Masekela in the band Jazz Epistles before leaving South Africa in 1962.

Jazz great Duke Ellington heard Ibrahim, bassist Johnny Gertze and drummer Makhaya Ntshoko playing and arranged a recording session for them, which resulted in the album *Duke Ellington presents the Dollar Brand Trio*. Ibrahim later played in the Newport Jazz festival in 1965, and landed a string of radio and recording contracts. He settled in New York, and played with some of jazz's big names including Don Cherry and Elvin Jones. In 1966, he substituted for Ellington and lead the Duke Ellington Orchestra on five occasions.

Ibrahim's music is hugely popular in Cape Town and his song *Manneburg*, which he made in partnership with saxophonist Basil Coetzee, is legendary among followers of South African jazz. Ibrahim is both strongly political and religious, aspects of his life which are reflected in his music.

In addition to performing at Cape Town's own North Sea Jazz Festival, he has performed at festivals in Montreux, Berlin, Montreal and many others. In recent years, he recorded with a 22-piece string orchestra and also wrote the soundtrack used in the film *Chocolat*.

Below: Adullah Ibrahim

Watson Mcoteli / PictureNET Africa

Calendar of Festivals and Events

The citizens of the Western Cape like to party, so it is no surprise that throughout the year there are a variety of festivals and other events designed to showcase the relaxed lifestyle of the Cape. Even sports events, although deadly serious during the duration of the event, get turned into parties afterwards. It is wise to check with tourism authorities to see if dates of events have changed, and if advanced booking is necessary. Also read the local media for other events.

A performer entertains the crowd at one of Cape Town's many music festivals

January
Cape Town New Year Carnival
The Cape Minstrels take to the streets, singing, dancing and playing music.
Standard Bank Cape Town Jazzathon
Four days of jazz.

February
Maynardville Shakespeare Festival
Famous for outdoor Shakespeare productions in summer.

Spier Summer Festival
Music, food and theatre.
Kirstenbosch Summer Sunset Concerts
Music in the gardens.

March
Cape Town Festival
A whole week of music, art and theatre.
Argus Pick 'n Pay Cycle Race
The largest of its kind in the world. Even though it is a cycle race, Cape Town is packed and very festive.

Copyright: South African Tourism

Cape Town New Year Carnival

April
North Sea Jazz Festival
Nederberg Wine Auction, Paarl
International and local buyers select the
Cape's best wines. It's fun and
fashionable too.
**Klein Karoo National Arts Festival,
Oudtshoorn**
Mainly in Afrikaans, but an interesting
aspect of South African culture.

May
Cape Town Gourmet Festival
A feast of fine cuisine, gourmet events
and street entertainment.

June
Greyton Winter Festival
Wine, food and arts.

July
Knysna Oyster Festival
Road marathons, cycle marathons,
music, wine and oysters straight from
the sea. The town is packed and everyone
has a party.

August
Clanwilliam Flower Festival
Flower displays and stalls of produce,
arts and crafts.

September
Hermanus Whale Festival
At the height of the whale watching
season. Arts and fun.
Stellenbosch Festival
Wine, food, arts and music.

October
Cape Town Flower Show
Flower displays and stalls.

November
**Die Burger Wine Festival,
Cape Town**
The biggest of its kind. More than
100 producers show off their wines.

December
Long Street Carnival
Several days of parties, dance
and art.

The North Sea Jazz Festival is one of Cape Town's biggest annual musical events

Impressions

Cape Town and the Western Cape are easy places to visit. There is excellent accommodation available, the road network is very good, air links are regular and reliable, and communication systems are good. As with the rest of South Africa, tourism in the Cape has boomed over the past decade, and many people have made it their business to ensure that tourism prospers as a viable and sustainable industry. The Western Cape is also easy to travel around, as distances are not as vast as those in other parts of the country.

Fishermen bring in the catch at Hout Bay Harbour

Climate

Cape Town and the southern Cape coast have a Mediterranean climate with warm to hot summers and mild to cool winters. Most of the rain falls in winter (*see p7*).

Elsewhere in South Africa most rainfall falls in summer. In many parts of the interior of the country, it can become very hot in summer, particularly in the Kruger National Park (KNP), Kalagadi Transfrontier Park and parts of KwaZulu-Natal.

Winter days in the interior are cool, but at night the temperature can fall below freezing. The coastal belt of KwaZulu-Natal is very humid in summer.

Tourists admire the view from the top of Table Mountain

Enjoying the sun and coffee at side-walk cafés at Camps Bay

School Holidays

Most South Africans take their annual holidays over Christmas or Easter, and more popular destinations are accordingly very busy. Although the crowds create an exciting atmosphere, tourists with some flexibility in their schedule might want to avoid these peak periods.

What to Take

All the major cities are well stocked with almost any item of clothing or equipment the average traveller might need. So should anything be forgotten, it can easily be replaced with something similar.

Health

Good medical care and hospitals are available throughout South Africa. Consult your doctor or a travel clinic about anti-malaria medication if you intend visiting the hot northern and northeastern parts of the country, particularly the Kruger National Park and the game reserves of northern KwaZulu-Natal.

All tap water is drinkable. Use sunscreen even in winter as South Africa has very high rates of ultraviolet radiation. *See also Directory on p181.*

Access for Disabled Persons

Although some buildings and public areas have been made user-friendly to disabled people, this is not widespread.

Larger airports have been designed or adapted to assist disabled people. *See also Directory on p188.*

Getting Around

• All the larger centres are linked by air, and rental cars are easily hired at airports.

- The Cape Town Council operates a bus service throughout the city. The routes are limited, and after dark buses are scarce.
- Public transport is not good, and in smaller centres or rural areas taxi services are poor. Cape Town has a fairly good suburban rail system, but it only serves a limited number of areas.
- It is best to make transport arrangements at the hotel or B&B, and to take advantage of local knowledge.
- Avoid the ubiquitous minibus taxis, unless you are prepared to endure bad driving and poorly maintained vehicles.

Tourists meandering through the V & A Waterfront

- Several reputable companies operate long-distance coaches between major centres, but be aware that distances can be intimidating. Cape Town, for example, is 1,500km (940 miles) from Johannesburg.
- There are tolls on major roads. Cash or credit cards are accepted.
- South Africa has an extensive rail system linking all the major centres. The luxurious Blue Train runs between Cape Town and Johannesburg, and is an easy way of seeing some of the countryside in comfort.

Self Drive

It is a good idea to carry a cell phone in case of a breakdown or some other emergency. Programme important numbers like that of the car rental company, the Automobile Association and your hotel into the phone so you can find help easily should you experience a breakdown.

South Africans are, as a rule, poor drivers so exercise caution on the roads.

Should the driver of the minibus taxi travelling in front of you activate the hazard lights on his vehicle, it means he is about to stop, whether it is legal or not, to collect or drop off passengers. Be alert. (On major routes drivers sometimes use their emergency flashers as a means of thanking you for allowing them to pass.)

Urban myth says that because of the crime rate people may feel unsafe and it is therefore acceptable to stop at a red traffic light late at night, and then continue on your way if the road is clear. It is not acceptable, and it is illegal. Wait for the green.

Crime

This subject is always at the top of most people's list of concerns. Parts of Cape Town, particularly the Cape Flats, have a high crime-rate, but authorities are working hard to find solutions to the problem. The best protection against criminals is common sense.
Tens of millions of South Africans use this tactic on a daily basis.

Take sensible precautions as you would anywhere else in the world, and, if in doubt, ask your hotel, B&B or tour guide for advice.

- If you are ever in the unfortunate position of having someone armed with a weapon attempt to steal your car or anything else, never ever resist. The situation is unlikely to arise but, if it does, let the thieves take whatever they want.
- Don't carry unnecessary cash or valuables, and do not leave cameras or bags on the seat of your car. Store them out of sight, preferably in the boot. Lock your doors.
- It is best to take tours to some areas rather than drive yourself. Again, ask advice. Avoid self-appointed 'guides' who approach you in the street.

And while it is important to be alert, remember the vast majority of tourists never experience crime so don't let the subject dominate your holiday.

Visiting Game Reserves

Never feed wild animals, whether in game reserves or not, because the animals begin to associate humans with food. This later causes conflict with humans, and authorities end up having to shoot problem-animals that are a threat. Human food also creates health problems in wild animals.

Follow these rules if you are visiting game reserves in other parts of South Africa:

- Don't get out of the car in Big Five game reserves as some species are potentially dangerous.
- If you encounter elephants while driving in a game reserve, always give them space to move off, and do not get between adults and babies. They are usually accustomed to cars and pose no threat, but it is best to give them space.
- If you have been walking through long grass, check your legs and arms for ticks afterwards. Several anti-tick sprays are available.
- Most mosquitoes start biting in the evening, so it is a good idea to wear long pants and long sleeves if you want to avoid getting bitten. Use mosquito repellents too.

Copyright: South African Tourism

Bontebok are endemic to the Western Cape

Language

South Africa has 11 official languages, and a list of useful phrases in all 11 languages would take up half this book.

English is widely spoken, and nearly all signage is in English. Other languages like Afrikaans, Zulu and Xhosa sometimes appear on signboards.

For the record, the 11 languages are English, Afrikaans, Ndebele, Northern Sotho (Pedi), Siswati, Southern Sotho, Tsonga, Tswana, Venda, Xhosa and Zulu. *For some useful words see p184.*

Etiquette

South Africans are generally friendly and welcoming towards tourists.

Most people are willing to offer advice and suggestions, and are happy to chat with foreigners about sport, politics or whatever subject seems appropriate.

A friendly "Hi, how are you?" will elicit an acknowledgement and probably the same question in response which forms a good platform for any conversation.

When meeting people, a handshake is a widely accepted form of greeting. Some Black people use a more complicated handshake, which involves the standard grip, and then, without releasing, slipping your hand around the other person's thumb, then returning to the traditional grasp.

Bathers in casualwear enjoy the water in front of colourful beach huts at St James – False Bay

Money

Travellers' cheques are accepted in most banks, and credit cards are used throughout the country. Credit cards are not accepted for fuel. Most banks issue a separate card for fuel purchases.

Clothing

The South African lifestyle is fairly casual. In summer, many people wear shorts, casual shirts and sandals, particularly at the coast and in game reserves. It is important to remember that Cape Town's winters can be very wet and windy, so if you are visiting between May and October, bring warm clothes and rain-gear.

For those unused to harsh sunlight, it is wise to remember to use sunscreen on legs and arms when wearing shorts and T-shirts.

Dress in good restaurants is slightly more formal, but jackets and ties are unnecessary unless on business.

Before you Leave

Visit the South African Tourism website to catch up on links to the latest shows, big sporting matches and other events that will add to the enjoyment of your trip.

South African Tourism
Tel: (011) 895 3000.
www.SouthAfrica.net

A worker having her lunch in Hout Bay

Cape Town

Sightseeing in Cape Town starts as you walk out the front door, because in good weather the famous Table Mountain is visible from almost every part of the city. And mountain views predominate throughout the Western Cape, forming a backdrop to beaches, vineyards, farms, towns and villages. The country's oldest buildings, museums and art galleries are also in the region, and together with the natural scenic beauty, form the basis for a thriving and growing tourism industry.

Bertram House
This pretty restored Georgian House is packed with period furniture, silverware, paintings and other interesting pieces.
Corner Orange St and Government Ave.
Tel: (021) 481 3940.
www.museums.org.za
Open: Tues–Thurs 10am–4pm.

Bo Kaap
The colourful and noisy Bo Kaap (Above, or Upper, Cape) district has a strong Muslim influence with residential homes, mosques and *halaal* butcheries squeezed next to each other on the slopes of Signal Hill.

Many buildings facing directly onto the cobbled streets have been renovated, and are brightly painted, creating a cheerful atmosphere. There are seven mosques in the neighbourhood, which was formerly known as the Malay Quarter because of its long history of being an area where many of the first slaves where housed.

Table Mountain and the popular Waterfront development

Some residents can trace their ancestry back to these slaves, and the neighbourhood has a very strong community spirit.

In the 1950s, the area nearly suffered the same fate as District Six but escaped demolition because the local residents banded together and managed to persuade the authorities to declare the area a national monument – a surprising victory considering the attitudes of the time.

In the 18th century, the Dutch used the Cape as a place of exile for Islamic leaders from their colonies in the East, and one, Tuan Guru, is buried in Bo Kaap. His tomb is one of about 18 *karamats* (Muslim shrines) in Cape Town which are visited by Muslims as a form of pilgrimage.

Bo Kaap Museum

This museum is housed in one of a row of colourfully painted, flat-roofed houses that were typical of parts of Cape Town in the 19th century. The museum recreates a Malay home of the period, and contains photographic essays as well as other displays that explain the history of Malays and Muslim people in the city.

Nearby is the Auwal Mosque, one of nine in the area. It was built in 1798, and was the first mosque in South Africa. It is still used every day. It is well worth making use of the tour companies that offer guided tours around the Bo Kaap.

Bo Kaap Museum
71 Wale St. Tel: (021) 481 3939.
Open: Mon–Sat 9.30am–4pm.
Admission charge.
Auwal Mosque
Dorp St.

The colourful Bo Kaap area

Cape Flats' Townships

Gugulethu, Kayalitsha, Crossroads and Nyanga are the home to the majority of Black Capetonians, and no visit to the region is complete without visiting these sprawling areas. In winter many of the poorer homes experience leaks, and sometimes even flooding when the driving rain gathers on poorly drained streets.

The nearby areas of Mitchell's Plain, Bonteheuwel and Heideveld were reserved for Coloured people during apartheid, and are home to hundreds of thousands of people.

Tours take in all the more politically significant areas as well as culturally important sites. Tour guides will happily stop at local restaurants or roadside cafés.

All the townships are within sight of Table Mountain, and make a startling contrast to the wealth concentrated on its slopes. Many townships tours also take in the Bo Kaap area and the District Six Museum.

Cape Town Tourism
Tel: (021) 426 4260 or 405 4500.

Townships

The townships of Nyanga, Guguletu, Khayalitsha and Crossroads sprawl across the sandy Cape Flats; conglomerations of thousands of corrugated iron and wood shacks squeezed next to small square brick houses. Here and there, larger, smarter houses tower over their neighbours, signs that a small amount of wealth is slowly creeping into these poor areas. The townships were designed by the apartheid state to house Black people who were only allowed into urban areas to supply labour, and even now, over a decade after the arrival of democracy, the legacy of that discrimination and deprivation is there for all to see.

Nearby the poor, formerly 'Coloured' areas of Bonteheuwel and Heideveld, and the slightly better-off Mitchell's Plain and Athlone areas, are also the products of apartheid. Although seldom known as townships, these areas were reserved for 'Coloureds', people of mixed race, and

were also deliberately neglected by the state and council authorities.

White people needed to apply for permission to enter townships, and similarly Black people needed permits to stay in urban areas.

Today the townships are open to all, but in most cases people move from these areas to better homes closer to the city when they can afford to do so. Very few people from formerly 'Whites-only' areas move to townships, and most White people have never even entered these areas where many of their fellow South Africans live.

Visitors to South Africa are often confused by the reference to 'townships' rather than suburbs or cities, which is not surprising as they are, in most cases, part of the same urban conurbations.

Although Guguletu is a big area with a large population, it is usually referred to as a township near Cape Town, and the same rule applies to KwaMashu near

galleries or museums. The experience, however, is well worth the time because Guguletu is a vastly different place to the suburbs of Cape Town, as are the streets of Nyanga and Khayalitsha.

Every city in South Africa has several neighbouring townships, usually hidden out of the way, and even small towns have their own 'townships'.

Durban, Soweto near Johannesburg and Mamelodi near Pretoria.

In recent years, the state has attempted to upgrade townships, and every day more and more people are provided with access to electricity, proper toilets and clean running water, but there is still a huge task to accomplish if everyone is to have even these basic services.

Many roads have been surfaced, and other infrastructure has been improved, but when winter rains and storms sweep the Cape Flats, many of the shacks in informal settlements are flooded.

Given this poverty, it may seem odd to treat townships as tourist attractions because, quite obviously, they are not

They are usually lively, friendly places where everyone seems to know everyone else, a characteristic often lacking in some of the formerly 'Whites only' suburbs in many South African cities.

Townships are home to the majority of urban South Africans, and they are an integral part of the fabric of society.

A tour to a township is an essential, entertaining and educational trip and should not be missed by any visitor to South Africa.

Cape Town Tourism
Tel: (021) 426 4260.
www.cape-town.org

Opposite: Gugulethu youths battle it out in a keenly contested game of pool in a township hall
Above: Two youngsters have a game of soccer in front of their Kayalitsha home
Left: Vicky's B&B is one of several in Kayalitsha where visitors can spend the night

Cape Town Holocaust Centre

The main focus of this somewhat sombre museum is the plight of European Jews during the rise of Nazism. There are also displays that tell the story of Jews in South Africa and their role in modern South Africa. The museum makes use of various multi-media techniques.
88 Hatfield St. Tel: (021) 462 5553.
www.museums.org.za
Open: Sun–Thurs 10am–5pm,
Fri 10am–1pm.
Closed: Sat & Jewish Holidays.
Free admission.

Next door is **The South African Jewish Museum.** This tells more of the story of South African Jews.
84 Hatfield St. Tel: (021) 465 1564.
www.sajewishmuseum.co.za.
Same opening hours as the centre above.
Admission charge.

Castle of Good Hope

This castle was built as a fort between 1666–1669, but it has fortunately never seen battle, and has slid into retirement by being turned into a museum. The building was designed in the shape of a five-pointed star complete with dank dungeons and passages beneath the battlements.

The museum contains the outstanding William Fehr Collection of paintings, furniture and other items dating back to the arrival of the first White settlers. For those who are interested in cutlasses, guns and other items of war, there is also a military museum housed in the castle.

Tours are conducted daily (call for

Castle of Good Hope – a fort which has never seen battle

times) and include a visit to the dark and damp dungeon under the main castle. There are two restaurants in the castle grounds.
Buitenkant St. Tel: (021) 787 1249
Open: daily 9am–4pm.
Admission charge.

Centre for the Book

The centre is a library designed to encourage reading among all South Africans. There is a wide variety of books and magazines available. It's all free of charge, but the books remain in the library, and they cannot be taken home.

The reading material is very varied, and provides an interesting insight into what young South Africans like to read. An internet café is also provided.
62 Queen Victoria St.
Tel: (021) 423 2669.
www.centreforthebook.co.za
Open: daily 8.30am–4.30pm.

A flower-seller in central Cape Town

Company's Gardens

The lush gardens with large old trees are right in the middle of the city, and provide easy access to a number of important museums and buildings, as well as offering some peace from the traffic.

The paths through these gardens meander past The Houses of Parliament, St Georges Cathedral, The South African National Gallery and The South African Museum. The Company's Gardens were not always in the middle of town, and were originally planted in 1652 by Jan van Riebeeck of the Dutch East India Company (VOC) to grow vegetables to supply passing company ships.

In good weather many people spend their lunch times or other free moments in the gardens enjoying the sun and chatting the time away.

The leafy Company's Gardens are used by many as a peaceful retreat

The gardens are open all day, but be cautious of 'street kids' who sometimes snatch bags or jewellery *(see box on p65)*.
Upper Adderley St.
Open: all day.

Cultural History Museum and Slave Lodge

The Dutch began importing slaves from the East, and from Mozambique and Madagascar, to the Cape in the 17th century, and some were housed in this building when they first arrived. It is one of the oldest buildings in the city, built in 1679, and has had a variety of uses. Besides housing slaves, it was used as a brothel, a post office, a jail, a library and was also once the Supreme Court. Now as a museum, there are displays and artefacts from Cape Town's history and, perhaps surprisingly, material from ancient Greece and the Far East.
49 Adderley St. Tel: (021) 461 8280.
www.museums.org.za
Open: daily 9.30am–4.30pm.
Admission charge.

District Six Museum

This is another museum that helps explain some of South Africa's history of racial discrimination, and includes comprehensive displays of pictures, maps, newspaper articles and other items.

District Six was a thriving community of mixed-race South Africans until the government of the day decided they should be moved out of sight of central Cape Town, and bulldozed the entire neighbourhood. The displays and writings reveal the deep hurt many people experienced after being evicted

The District Six Museum tells the story of a whole community that was destroyed

from their homes and watching them being bulldozed down. Some of the workers at the museum used to live in the area, and all have sad stories to tell of how their homes were destroyed. For years the land stood vacant except for a few mosques, but people are now slowly moving back into District Six. Tours can be arranged.

25A Buitekant St. Tel: (021) 461 8745.
www.districtsix.co.za
Open: Mon–Sat 9am–4pm. Closed: Sun.

Gold of Africa Museum

Gold has played an important role in the history of South Africa, however, this unique museum contains gold items and artwork from all over Africa. The large and unusual collection of more than 350 items includes gold masks and animals, and other artwork from Ghana, Mali, Senegal and elsewhere in West Africa. Goldsmiths from Ghana and Mali are particularly skilled, and many examples of their 19th and 20th century works are displayed in the museum.

The building which houses the museum was built in 1783, and is an important architectural landmark. The façade on the building next door has remained unchanged since the 1820s.

Museum staff run workshops in gold jewellery-making techniques, and the shop sells a variety of jewellery and other mementos as well as some excellent wines.

The Gold of Africa Museum contains exquisite examples of African Gold jewellery

Shopping at Greenmarket Square in the centre of the city of Cape Town

Martin Melk House, 96 Strand St.
Tel: (021) 405 1540.
www.goldofafrica.co.za
Open: Mon–Sat 9.30am–5pm.
Closed: Sun. Free admission.

Greenmarket Square

This cobbled fleamarket, set in a square in the middle of the city, is a hive of activity as hawkers and stall-holders display their wares which include curios, clothing and odds and ends. Some carvings come from as far away as Ivory Coast and Nigeria, but others are much more mundane including drinks-holders with pictures of Table Mountain glued to the plastic. Experienced fleamarket shoppers will soon find the bargains. There are lots more formal shops in the area and many restaurants.
Corner Burg St and Longmarket St.
Open: Mon–Sat.

Groot Constantia

Most tourists in Cape Town end up visiting Groot Constantia sooner or later, and seldom regret the trip. Not only is this one of Cape Town's most elegant buildings and the oldest wine estate in the country, but it is also set in magnificent grounds which are alone worth the visit. Established by Cape Governor Simon van der Stel in 1685, the estate produces some of the best wines in the Cape. Napoleon Bonaparte's time in exile was made a little easier by supplies of wine from this estate!

The Manor House Cultural Museum is well worth a visit too. There are two restaurants, and in summer many people order pre-prepared picnics from them and sit in the tranquil gardens and admire the views.
Groot Constantia Rd.
Tel: (021) 794 5128.
www.grootconstantia.co.za
Open: daily 10am–5pm.
Admission charge to museum.

Groote Kerk

This ornate old church was originally built in 1703 but was rebuilt in 1841. It is now hemmed in by more modern buildings that detract from its ornate design. The interior of the Groote Kerk ('big church') is appropriately grand with a huge pipe organ and teak pulpit.
Upper Adderly St.
Tel: (021) 461 7044.
Open: Mon–Fri 10am–2pm.
Service Sunday.

Houses of Parliament

These stately buildings were opened in 1885, and have had various bits and pieces added on over the years. Much of South Africa's modern political history has had its origins here, and tour guides help explain the more significant events, as well as adding interesting titbits about some of the buildings' occupants over the years.

Parliament St. Tel: (021) 403 3683.
www.parliament.gov.za
Open: Mon–Fri. Tours on the hour from 9am–12pm. Booking required.
Free admission.

Hout Bay

Some residents of Hout Bay proudly view themselves as 'separate' from Cape Town, and at one stage even printed a fake passport bearing the inscription 'Republic of Hout Bay'. Despite this, Hout Bay is part of greater Cape Town. There are fantastic views from Chapman's Peak Drive, which begins on the edge of the town. All the way up the drive there are phenomenal views across the bay, and further along, as the road winds along the mountainside, there are also great views of the wide expanse of Noordhoek Beach. A toll is charged for vehicles using Chapman's Peak Drive.

Hout Bay is a laid-back holiday town with a variety of hotels and bars which are good places for sundowners. The Mariners Wharf is a good place for fresh seafood and old-fashioned fish and chips.

Two youngsters earning pocket money by selling small gifts at Hout Bay fishing harbour

Irma Stern Museum

Some of Irma Stern's best expressionist works are displayed here, as well her personal collection of international art.

Much of her work was considered to be groundbreaking and ahead of its time for South African audiences. Stern (1904–1996) lived in the house for nearly 40 years, and her studio has been kept as it was when she worked there. The museum sometimes hosts exhibitions of other artists too.
Cecil Rd, Rosebank. Tel: (021) 685 5686.
www.irmastern.co.za
Open: Tues–Sat 10am–5pm.
Small admission charge.

Iziko-SA National Gallery

South Africa's premier art gallery was started in 1871 with just 45 paintings donated by Thomas Bayley. Today the collection has grown dramatically, although there has been a move away from international art towards works from Africa. Despite this in part being due to a desire to display more African arts, the high cost on international art has also influenced exhibitions.

Some of the permanent displays include work by British, French, Dutch and Flemish masters. The work of the New English Art Club and the Bloomsbury Group are also represented. There are comprehensive displays of South African and international art from different periods including paintings, beadwork, sculptures, ceramics and textiles. Some exhibitions are changed regularly, but others are permanent.
Government Ave, Company's Gardens.
Tel: (021) 456 1628.
Open: Tues–Sun 10am–5pm. Closed: Mon.
www.museums.org.za
Admission charge.

Iziko-SA National Gallery – South Africa's oldest art gallery

Koopmans-de Wet House

The museum has been designed to look like a furnished 19th century house, which is exactly what it is. There is a good collection of old furniture and Delft and Japanese ceramics, as well as silverware and paintings. The home used to belong to Maria Koopmans-de Wet, a wealthy socialite.

The façade on the outside of the building was designed by one of Cape Town's foremost 19th century architects Louis Thibault and sculptor Anton Anreith.

35 Strand St. Tel: (021) 481 3935.
www.museums.org.za
Open: Tues–Thur 9.30am–4.30pm.
Admission charge.

Long Street Baths

These Turkish baths are a famous Cape Town landmark and were built in 1908. There is also a massage room and a swimming pool. Men and women use the baths on alternate days.

Corner Long St. and Orange St.
Tel: (021) 400 3302.
Open: Women – Mon & Thur 9am–8pm,
Sat 9am–6pm. Men – Tue, Wed & Fri
9am–6pm, Sun 8am–12pm.
Admission charge.

Lwandle Cultural Village

The village has an interesting crafts market, and the local museum built in a migrant labour hostel tells the history of people who travelled to the Cape from rural areas in search of work. Local residents arrange tours of the township.

Old Community Halls, Vulindela St,
Lwandle, off the N2 near Somerset West.
Tel: (021) 845 6119.

Maynardville

Maynardville hosts plays and experimental theatre all year round but the highlight is between December and February when Shakespearean plays are produced outdoors. The popular performances are a great attraction, and people bring picnics to enjoy while watching the theatre. Maynardville also hosts the Community Chest Carnival in February to raise money for charities. The complex has been running for almost half a century.

Corner Church St and Wolfe St.
Tel: (021) 421 7695.
www.artscape.co.za
Call for details of performances.

Colourful beadwork is sold in many markets

Michaelis Collection

Among Cape Town's most prized art treasures, the internationally acclaimed Michaelis Collection contains works by Rembrandt, Frans Hals, Jan van Goyen and other 16th and 17th century Dutch masters. Flemish artists are also well represented, including works by Anthony van Dyck. Most were donated by Sir Max Michaelis in 1914, and are displayed in the Old Town House building which was built in 1755 and was once used as the City Hall.
Greenmarket Square. Tel: (021) 481 3933. Open: Mon–Fri 10am–5pm, Sat 10am–4pm. Closed: Sun. www.museums.org.za Entry by donation.

Newlands Cricket Ground

Newlands is regarded by cricket fans as one of the prettiest cricket grounds in the world, and regular tours are conducted through the grounds. Although the tours are interesting, it is definitely more exciting to watch a real game!

146 Campground Rd. Tel: (021) 657 2003. Tours: Mon–Fri. Tel: (021) 686 2150. www.newlandstours.co.za

Newlands Rugby Stadium

Both the cricket and rugby stadiums are known simply as 'Newlands', despite the fact that both are now sponsored by financial institutions who demand that their name be included in the title of the grounds. Newlands is one of the oldest rugby test venues in the world, the first test being played in 1890. The tours are

UNIVERSITIES OF THE WESTERN CAPE

The University of Cape Town (UCT) has a fine reputation for producing some of South Africa's best academics, business people, doctors and scientists and, as a bonus, has a magnificent setting on the slopes of Table Mountain. Beautiful buildings on campus add to the grandeur.

Not far away in the winelands, the University of Stellenbosch is no less beautiful, its stately white halls and Cape Dutch architecture surrounded by leafy oak trees with blue-grey mountain ranges in the background. For years Stellenbosch produced the cream of Afrikaner society, although the university has moved with the times and now caters for all South Africans.

Despite not being blessed with the same scenic splendour as the previous two institutions, the University of the Western Cape has also played its role in society, and in the 1990s was a hotbed of student activism and resistance to apartheid. Although originally created during apartheid for Coloured people only, the university now too is open to all, and is a vibrant source of ideas and innovative thinking.

University of Cape Town (UCT)

The grand Rhodes Memorial – a tribute to Cecil John Rhodes

interesting but, as with the cricket stadium, it is much more exciting to watch a big game, particularly when the ground is packed to its capacity of 50,000 people.

11 Boundary Rd. Tel: (021) 659 4600.
www.wprugby.com
Tours: Mon–Fri. Tel: (021) 686 2150.
www.newlandstours.co.za
Free admission.

If visiting Newlands, also pop into the **SARFU Rugby Museum** – a small museum which is sometimes included in the stadium tour.

Sports Science Institute, Boundary Rd.
Tel: (021) 686 2151.
Open: Mon–Fri 8.30am–5.30pm.
Free admission.

Pan African Market

This market is pretty much 'Africa under one roof'. People from countries as far away as Mali, Nigeria, Cameroon and Ethiopia sell their work here and they, and other migrants, gather at the Kalakuta Republic Book Café to chat, have a meal or listen to poetry readings.

There are more than 30 stalls at the market. The West and Central African fetish masks are particularly good, but it is necessary to bargain to get competitive prices.

76 Long St. Tel: (021) 426 4478.
www.panafrican.co.za
Open: daily 9am–6pm.

Rhodes Memorial

The memorial, designed by Sir Herbert Baker *(see Architecture on p23–5)* has lovely views over Cape Town. Cecil John Rhodes made a fortune in the Kimberley diamond rush, and had a grandiose plan to expand the British Empire's possessions in Africa all the way from Cape to Cairo. He wanted to link all these countries by a single railway line too. Although he never succeeded, his influence in southern Africa was considerable, and Rhodesia (now Zimbabwe) was named after him.

He also served as a prime minister of the Cape. There is a restaurant at the memorial, and zebras and wildebeest in graze in the grounds. There are also lovely walks through the grounds.

Groote Schuur Estate, Klipper Rd.
Tel: (021) 689 9151.

Rondevlei Nature Reserve

Rondevlei (meaning 'round lake') is a small nature reserve surrounded by human development, but is an important wetland. A large number of birds occur here, and the reserve is the only place that you might be lucky enough to see hippos that are not confined to small enclosures.

Several hippos were reintroduced to the lakes, and are the first wild hippos to live in the Cape Peninsula for several hundred years. All the original animals were shot by early settlers.

Fisherman's Walk Rd, Zeekkoeivlei.
Tel: (021) 706 0842.
Check opening times, as they vary winter to summer. Admission charge.

Rust en Vreugd

The gallery includes paintings from the William Fehr collection as well as work by Thomas Baines, Thomas Bowler and others. The building is a carefully restored 18th century Cape Town house, and is an excellent example of Cape Dutch architecture.

78 Buitenkant St.
Tel: (021) 465 3628.
www.museums.org.za
Open: Tue–Thur 8.30am–4.30 pm.
Admission charge.

Noon-day explosion is heard from Signal Hill

Signal Hill and Lions Head

After Table Mountain, these are two of the most famous landmarks in Cape Town, and, best of all, they both provide excellent views of their big sister. They also provide great views of central Cape Town, The Waterfront, the beaches at Camps Bay and Clifton, and Robben Island. They also help emphasise the sheer scale of Table Mountain soaring over the city.

Every day Signal Hill echoes to the sound of gunfire, but it is entirely harmless, and is useful for checking that your watch is accurate. The Noon Gun, an old cannon, is fired from Signal Hill with an explosion that is audible all over Cape Town. The tradition dates back to 1806 when the Noon Gun was used to allow ships in the harbour to set their clocks accurately. Once you have checked your watch, the nearby restaurant is a good place for a bite to eat or a drink.
Military Rd, Signal Hill.
Tel: (021) 787 1257.
Open: Mon–Sat. Free admission.

TABLE MOUNTAIN NATIONAL PARK

Nearly every mountain between Table Mountain and Cape Point, a distance of some 60km (37 miles), falls into the Table Mountain National Park (formerly Cape Peninsula National Park). The park is the richest botanical area for its size on Earth, and a variety of mammals, birds and fish are also protected. It is an unusual national park in that it falls entirely within a metropolitan area.

There are hundreds of kilometres of hiking trails along the mountains and beaches, although there is limited accommodation within the park and at Cape Point. Most people merely stay in urban areas and walk straight onto beaches or the mountains.
Tel: (021) 701 8692.
www.tmnp.co.za

Camps Bay with Lions Head in the background

Simon's Town Museum

This museum reveals the history of
Simon's Town which for decades has
been South Africa's largest naval base.
There are displays and exhibits relating to
the South African War, South Africa's role
in both world wars and local history. A
section of the museum explains the
history of the local Malay population.
Court Rd, Simon's Town.
Tel: (021) 786 3046.
Open: Mon–Fri 9am–4pm, Sat
10am–4pm & Sun 11am–4pm.
Closed: Christmas Day & Good Friday.

South African Maritime Museum

Appropriately situated at the V & A
Waterfront, this museum examines
the shipping history of Cape Town,
and to a lesser degree, South Africa.
There is a large collection of models, and
children will enjoy the 'Discovery Cove'.
Entry includes access to two naval vessels
moored at the nearby quayside.
Dock Rd, V & A Waterfront.
Tel: (021) 405 2880.
www.museums.org.za
Open: daily 10am–4.45pm.
Admission charge.

South African Museum & Planetarium

South Africa's oldest museum is a
treasure trove of animal exhibits, insects,
whales, fossils, rock art, pottery, and just
about anything that lives, or has ever
lived, in southern Africa. The museum is
extensive, with thousands of specimens
on display – and the storerooms contain
a further one and a half million
specimens of scientific importance.

Some of the more unusual displays are
the Linton Panel, which was discovered

PHOTOGRAPHY

Cape Town and the Western Cape offer
hundreds of great photo opportunities,
but it is important to remember that African
light is usually fairly harsh. The best times
for photography are usually early morning,
in summer before 10am, or late afternoon.
A skylight filter is useful (if your camera lens
accepts add-on filters) for removing some haze
and glare. A polarising filter is useful in
highlighting clouds or deepening blues. Dust is
also often a problem, particularly in the Karoo,
so clean the camera lens regularly with
compressed air or a photographic lens brush.

There are photographic opportunities aplenty
throughout the Cape Peninsula

in a rock shelter in the Eastern Cape,
containing San rock art, and the
Lydenburg Heads, some of the earliest
African sculptures. Some fossils at the
museum date back more than 700,000
years. In the Whale Well, there is,
among other displays, a complete
20m-long skeleton of a blue whale.

The museum was founded in 1825,
and scientists working for the museum

since then have gathered huge numbers of exhibits that contribute significantly to our knowledge of the history of southern Africa.

South African Museum
25 Queen Victoria St. Tel: (021) 481 3800.
www.museums.org.za
Open: daily 10am–5pm. Closed:
Christmas Day & Good Friday.
Admission charge.

The Planetarium
Shows: Mon–Fri 2pm & Sat 12pm,
1pm & 2.30pm. Also Tues 8pm.

St George Street Mall

This pedestrian mall runs right through the middle of Cape Town, and provides easy access to many tourist attractions. There are a good number of shops suitable for browsing. A variety of artists, buskers and freelance salesmen frequent the mall which usually has a lively atmosphere. It is a good place to grab a cup of coffee or tea and watch some of Cape Town's street life.

St George's Cathedral

The cathedral was designed by Sir Herbert Baker *(see Architecture on p23–5)* and built in 1901. Archbishop Desmond Tutu officiated here in the 1980s, and on several occasions police broke up meetings at the cathedral on the grounds that they were political gatherings and not religious services.
1 Wale St. Tel: (021) 424 7360.
Open: Mon–Fri 10am–2pm.
Open Sun for services.

CAPE TOWN GRAFFITI

Cape Town has an energetic community of graffiti artists, many of whom were at their peak during the last years of apartheid. Two gems: while Winnie Madikizela-Mandela was on trial for kidnapping an activist, a charge of which she was later found guilty, a Cape Town wall was emblazoned with 'Winnie is in the Poo'.

On another occasion during the 'people's protests' against apartheid, riot people used a water cannon to douse protesters with jets of water dyed purple so they could be identified and arrested later. The next morning the graffiti read 'The Purple shall Govern' a play on the popular 'The People shall Govern' slogan of the day.

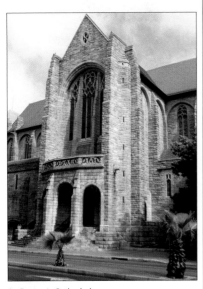
St George's Cathedral

Table Mountain and Cableway

Hundreds of thousands of people have climbed Table Mountain, but perhaps the best description of the view from the top was written more than 180 years ago.

"The view", wrote botanist William Burchell in 1822 after being inspired to climb Table Mountain "…is singularly grand."

For just under four centuries the 1,087m- (3,532ft-) high mountain has been the focal point of Cape Town, influencing weather patterns and even people's attitudes.

It forms a bold northern front of a high range stretching 60km (96 miles) to Cape Point. The mountain slopes and ravines offer dozens of walks and climbs from the easy to the severe, while the cable car transports passengers to the summit's viewing platforms and restaurants.

Cable station
Tel: (021) 424 8181.
www.tablemountain.co.za
Opening hours vary according to season. Also check weather conditions as the cable station may close in bad weather.

The cableway to the top of Table Mountain is one of Cape Town's most popular attractions

Telkom Exploratium

The exploratium has all sorts of electrical and interactive fun and games. There are racing cars, aeroplanes and science displays that will have lovers of video games entertained for hours.
Union Castle House, V & A Waterfront.
Tel: (021) 419 5957.
www.exploration.co.za
Admission charge.

The Joan St Leger Lindbergh Arts Foundation

The foundation has restored four houses designed and built by Sir Herbert Baker (1862–1946). There are displays of old books and other Africana, as well as old newspaper clippings with stories relating to the area. In summer, concerts are held in the gardens.
18 Beach Rd, Muizenberg.
Tel: (021) 788 2795.
Open: Mon–Fri. 9am–3.30 pm.
Call for concert and event times. Free admission, but there is charge for concerts.

The Red Shed Craft Workshop

This indoor market has a huge variety of goods on offer. There are African carvings, handmade clothes, beadwork, paintings and many other items.
Victoria Wharf, V & A Waterfront.
Tel: (021) 408 7600.
Open: daily 9am–9pm.

Thunder City

Combat jets have a strange attraction for many people, and Thunder City is one of the few places in the world where tourists can go for a flip in one of these aircraft. The flights are for the rich only, but even if you can't afford a sub-sonic flight over the Cape Peninsula, the aircraft and other memorabilia can be viewed at close range when they are not flying. Thunder City has an English Electric Lightning, BAe Buccaneer and Hawker Hunter on display.
Cape Town International Airport.
Tel: (021) 934 8007.
www.thundercity.com
Open: Mon–Sun 9am–5pm.
Admission charge.

Tokai Arboretum and Manor House

There are lovely walks through the estate which is a national heritage site. Although many of the trees planted on the estate by Joseph Lister in 1885 are not indigenous, they are protected by law. Lister planted the trees, which come from all over the world, to see if any were suitable for large-scale cultivation in the Cape. There are good walks and mountain biking trails. There is also a restaurant, and the historic manor house is worth a visit.
Tokai Rd, Tokai. Tel: (021) 712 7471.
Open: daily 7am–7pm.

Combat jets on display at Thunder City

Two Oceans Aquarium

Walking through long, cool, dimly lit passages of the aquarium, watching seaweeds gently swaying in the current, and fish, sharks and other marine creatures swimming by, is the nearest one can get to diving without donning scuba gear. The Two Oceans Aquarium is a modern, 'state of the art' aquarium designed to entertain and educate visitors at the same time.

Marine creatures from all along the South African coast live in the aquarium's tanks, and shoals of deep-sea fish, sharks, rays, coral reef displays, turtles, seals and penguins go about their daily lives unconcerned by all the spectators.

For those who are prepared to get wet, there are interactive displays where children can touch some sea creatures, and qualified divers can even arrange to swim in the tank where the sharks live.

The aquarium is home to fish and marine life from both the South Africa's warm east coast and the cold west coast waters.
Dock Rd, V & A Waterfront.
Tel: (021) 418 3823.
www.aquarium.co.za
Open: daily 9.30am–6pm.
Admission charge.

WATER MUSIC

From May to November, the Two Oceans Aquarium runs a series of Sunday concerts next to their predator exhibit. Nobody has been fed to the sharks for applauding at inappropriate moments, and the fee includes entry to the aquarium. The musicians play against a backdrop of the tank with sharks swimming by. Call for times and details of the performances.

Underwater splendour at the Two Oceans Aquarium

The hugely popular V & A Waterfront

Victoria and Alfred Waterfront (V & A Waterfront)

The Waterfront receives more visitors in a year than any other single place in the country. It is a vast complex of hugely popular shops, curio stores, restaurants, cinemas and museums. Many of the restaurants overlook the harbour, and in good weather the walkways and piers fill up with people enjoying a drink or a meal while watching activity in the working harbour. The complex provides endless entertainment and shopping for the whole family, some of whom spend the entire day wandering between the stores, movies and restaurants. Several hotels are also part of the complex.

Ferries leave from here for Robben Island and cruises to Cape Point. There are also boats that make fantastic 'sunset' cruises along the Bantry Bay, Clifton Beach and Camps Bay coast.

Other boats cruise to Cape Point, weather permitting.
Tel: (021) 408 7600.
Open: daily.

Wine Estates

Although the next four places are vineyards with excellent wine cellars, they are also historical sites in their own right and are fascinating places even for those who have no interest in wine.

Buitenverwagting

Buitenverwagting means 'beyond expectations', and looking at the views it's easy to see why the first settlers were so impressed. It's a great place to picnic under the oaks. There are also lovely walks through the estate.
Klein Constantia Rd. Tel: (021) 794 5190.
www.buitenverwagting.co.za
Open: Mon–Fri 9am–5pm,
Sat 9am–1pm.

Constantia Uitsig

Once again, lovely views and good food.
Spaanschemat River Rd.
Tel: (021) 794 6500.
www.uitsig.co.za
Open: Mon–Sat 9am–6pm.

Klein Constantia Estate

Klein means 'little' and this estate
was once a little part of the Constantia,
farm. Like its big sister Groot (big)
Constantia there are various historic
buildings on the farm.
Klein Constantia Rd.
Tel: (021) 794 5188.
www.kleinconstantia.com
Open: Mon–Fri 9am–5pm,
Sat 9am–1pm.

Steenberg Vineyards

Built in 1682, the farmhouse is a
national monument. There is a world-
class restaurant and an excellent golf
course next door.
Steenberg Rd, Tokai.
Tel: (021) 713 2211.
www.steenberg-vineyards.co.za
Open: Mon–Fri 9am-5pm, Sat 9am–1pm.

World of Birds

The World of Birds has more than 300
exotic and local birds housed in walk-
through enclosures. Many of the birds
are victims of collisions with power
lines, fences and cars. There are a lot of
spotted eagle owls which watch passing
toes peeking out of sandals with
considered sagacity! It's a great visit
for children and adults alike.
Valley Rd, Hout Bay.
Tel: (021) 790 2730.
www.worldofbirds.org.za
Open: Mon–Sun 9am–5pm.
Admission charge.

Vines and mountains complete a typical Cape scene at Constantia

Many old houses in the Cape have been carefully restored

Whether you want to shop for African carvings, colourful T-shirts or old books, indulge in an all night party, enjoy a quiet cup of coffee or simply wander along watching the passing parade, Long Street has something for everyone.

Long Street, rather appropriately, runs for some 20 blocks along the edge of the city centre, starting in the business area near the Cape Town International Convention Centre and ending at the fun part near Kloof Road.

Some of Cape Town's best-known shops are in Long Street, and have been there for years, but some of the clubs and bars open and close down more erratically as the owners decide to head for greener pastures or go surfing in Bali or Brazil.

Clarkes Bookshop *(211 Long St, Tel: (021) 423 5739)* is one of South Africa's most famous bookshops, and has a comprehensive range of African and other antiquarian books. They also stock valuable old maps and hand-coloured prints dating back to the 19th century. Early explorers and artists left a rich heritage of work that provides an invaluable insight into the South African people and wildlife of the 17th, 18th and 19th centuries.

There are several other good bookstores dotted along the street.

Beezy Bailey, one of South Africa's well-known and innovative artists has a shop *(4 Long St, Corner Buiten St, Tel: (021) 423 4195),* and he has transformed the façade of the building into a work of art in its own right.

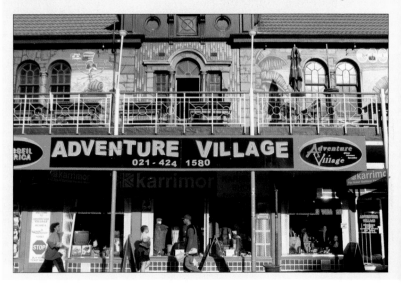

There are any number of restaurants, bars and clubs along the street. Indian, Thai, Turkish, Italian and dozens of other types of food are available including whole roast chickens from Fontana Roastery *(166 Long St, Tel: (021) 424 7233)*. Fontana is a legend among South African party-goers because the store stayed open all night long before any others were bold enough to do so.

Various other art stores can be found elsewhere along the street. Some of the art might have appalled John Constable or Rembrandt van Rijn, but it's often lively and colourful and is typical of the vibrant nature of this part of Cape Town.

Clothing stores vary, but they too, like some of the art, are usually not for the conservative. Purple velvet dresses hang on rails alongside fake-fur jackets and 'Mandela style' multi-coloured African casual shirts.

The fun at bars and clubs tends to start late because on Fridays and Saturdays, in particular, many stay open until three or four in the morning.

A favourite bar in Cape Town is, oddly enough, called Jo'burg, where nobody minds how rich or poor you are just so long as you are there to have fun *(218 Long St, Tel: (021) 422 0142)*.

Most of the accommodation in Long Street is aimed at backpackers and budget-travellers.

In the unlikely event that Long Street becomes too boring, nearby Kloof Nek and Kloof roads are also full of shops, restaurants and bars.

Opposite: Long Street is the centre of a funky, young-at-heart part of Cape Town
Above: A hawker tries to tempt a young couple into buying his flowers
Left: Catching an early morning cup of coffee after the previous night's party

Walk: Central Cape Town

Perhaps the best way to get a feel of Cape Town is to take a walk through the central city, and to visit some of the many historical buildings, museums and the leafy Company's Gardens. The central city is usually quite safe, but it is still wise to be alert when out walking.

Allow a full day. This is a short walk, but there is a lot to do along the way including having lunch at any one of the many cafés or restaurants. Start at the South African Museum and Planetarium, 25 Queen Victoria Street.

African fabrics sold at the market

1 The South African Museum and Planetarium

The museum has extensive displays explaining South Africa's natural and social history, and is one of the best in the country. As you leave the Museum, the Iziko-South African National Gallery is on the right, across the lawns of the Company's Gardens. Next to the Gallery is the Old Synagogue, the Jewish Museum and the Holocaust Centre. *For more information on all these museums, galleries and buildings, see What to see in Cape Town on pp38–60.*

The blue whale may grow as long as 31 metres – this skeleton is in the National Museum

The popular Greenmarket Square flea market

2 Company's Gardens

Meander through the lovely gardens where Jan van Riebeeck and his staff grew vegetables in 1854. Today the gardens are graced with large, shady trees where grey squirrels (an alien species which arrived with the Dutch) scamper around.

As you walk through the gardens, the Tuynhuis, the State President's residence dating from 1700, is on the right – as are the Houses of Parliament.

3 St George's Cathedral and Cultural History Museum

As you leave the Company's Gardens, St George's Cathedral is on your left. On the right, diagonally across Wale Street, is the Cultural History Museum (49 Adderley St), which is housed in the former Slave Lodge built in 1660. This is one of the oldest buildings in South Africa.
Head up Wale Street to the intersection of St George's Street Mall.

STREET KIDS

Street kids are homeless youngsters who live in the streets of South Africa's larger cities. Many abuse drugs, and in particular sniff glue. Sadly some of these children resort to crime as a means of surviving.

They usually work in groups with one child distracting the victim as the others snatch bags, necklaces or any other item they can grab. Many also beg at traffic lights. It is best to resist giving them money because it is often used to buy glue. There are several organisations and shelters that try to offer these children better lives.

Ndebele dolls are popular mementos for tourists

4 Rhodes House and St George's Street Mall

Rhodes House is an ornately decorated building that was once the Cape Town headquarters of the influential De Beers diamond company. Continue along St George's Mall, a pedestrian walkway lined with shops, stalls and buskers.

The Mall continues for quite a long way, but once you have browsed enough, turn into Shortmarket Street (it forms a T-junction with the Mall) and enter Greenmarket Square.

5 Greenmarket Square

This cobbled square is packed with stalls selling everything from African masks to socks and kaftans (Mon–Sat). Visit the Old Town House which was built in 1755 and houses the Michaelis Art collection of 17th century Dutch and Flemish painters, including Rembrandt van Rijn.

From the Old Townhouse, cross Greenmarket Square, and turn left into Shortmarket Street, and left again into Long Street.

6 Pan African Market

On the right-hand side of Long Street, you will find the Pan African Market (76 Long St) which is packed with art and curios from all over Africa.

Continue down Long Street, and turn left into the Church Street Mall.

7 Church Street Mall

The Church Street Mall is lined with antique shops, art stores and cafés.

This a good place to have a drink while you wait for a taxi or rest your feet before heading back to the hotel or B&B.

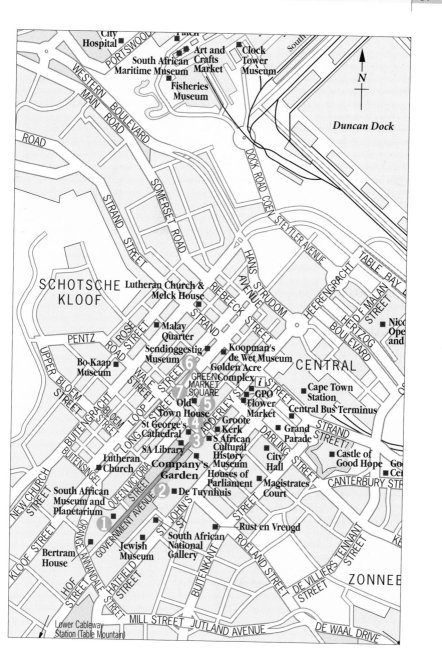

City Hospital
PORTSWOOD
Patch
Art and Crafts Market
Clock Tower Museum
South African Maritime Museum
Fisheries Museum
WESTERN BOULEVARD
MAIN ROAD
ROAD
SOMERSET ROAD
STRAND STREET
Duncan Dock
DOCK ROAD
COEN STEYTLER AVENUE
N

SCHOTSCHE KLOOF
Lutheran Church & Melck House
RIEBECK AVENUE
HANS STRIJDOM AVENUE
HEERENGRACHT
TABLE BAY
PENTZ
ROSE STREET
STRAND STREET
Malay Quarter
Sendinggestig Museum
Koopman's de Wet Museum
CENTRAL
D F MALAN STREET
HERTZOG BOULEVARD
Nico Ope and
Bo-Kaap Museum
UPPER BLOEM STREET
BUITENGRACHT STREET
BLOEM STREET
LOOP STREET
LONG STREET
WALE STREET
Golden Acre
GREEN MARKET SQUARE Complex
6
7 5
Old Town House
St George's Cathedral
4
3
i
GPO
Flower Market
Cape Town Station
Central Bus Terminus
ADDERLEY STREET
STRAND STREET
Groote Kerk
S African Cultural History Museum
DARLING STREET
Grand Parade
Castle of Good Hope
Go Cer
BUITENSINGEL
SA Library
Lutheran Church
Company's Garden
QUEEN VICTORIA STREET
2
De Tuynhuis
Houses of Parliament
City Hall
Magistrates Court
CANTERBURY STR
NEW CHURCH STREET
South African Museum and Planetarium
1
GOVERNMENT AVENUE
ORANGE ANNANDALE STREET
ST JOHN'S ST
Rust en Vreugd
ROELAND STREET
DE VILLIERS TENNANT STREET
KLOOF STREET
Bertram House
HOF STREET
HATFIELD STREET
Jewish Museum
South African National Gallery
BUITENKANT STREET
ZONNEE

Lower Cableway Station (Table Mountain)
MILL STREET
JUTLAND AVENUE
DE WAAL DRIVE

Tour: V & A Waterfront

The V & A Waterfront is hugely popular, and more than 20 million people use the complex of shops, cinemas, restaurants and varied tourist attractions annually. Much of the area used to be part of the harbour, and many of the buildings date back to the 19th century. One of the area's attractions is that it is part of a functioning harbour.

This walking tour will not take very long, unless of course you decide to meander off and visit the many shops and restaurants in the Waterfront Complex. The Clock Tower is a good place to start – the V & A Waterfront Information office is also in this building.

V & A Waterfront with Table Mountain in the background

The 1882 Clock Tower

The Clock Tower
The red and grey Clock Tower is visible from many parts of the Waterfront, and is a useful landmark when attempting to get around the vast complex. It was the original Port Captain's office, and was completed in 1882. The tower allowed the Port Captain a good view of activity in the harbour.

Cross the Swing Bridge (near the departure point for the Robben Island ferries).

Port Captain's New Office
This is right in front of you as you cross the bridge. It was built in 1904.

Robinson Dry Dock
The dock is still operational and dates back to 1882. Vessels are moored in the dock, large gates are lowered into place and the water in the dock is pumped out. After the ship has been repaired, the gates are opened and the ship floats out into the bay again.

V & A Waterfront at night

South African Maritime Museum

This is situated next to the Robinson Dry Dock and houses displays that tell the history of Cape Town. There are two ships moored nearby that are also part of the Museum (*see details in 'What to see section' on p54*).

Breakwater Prison

If you stand with your back towards the Dry Dock and the Clock Tower, the building that housed the old Breakwater Prison is on the far side of Dock Road in front of you. It was built in 1860, and cheap labour was provided by the convicts to help build the harbour. Ironically the building is now the home of the University of Cape Town's Graduate School of Business.

Follow Dock Road towards the Victoria Basin.

Time Ball Tower

This is on the corner before Dock Road turns sharply to the left. This tower was built in 1894, and was used to enable shipping captains to check their clocks for accuracy. The Noon Gun on Signal Hill was fired according to the time determined at the tower. The tower was inoperative for many years before being fully restored.

There are various other buildings of historical significance.
Details available from:
Cape Tourism Office
V & A Waterfront,
Tel: (021) 405 4500.

Robben Island

Robben Island was used as a prison for almost 400 years, and occupies an almost mythical position in South African history, largely because it was here that Nelson Mandela, among many others, was imprisoned. Today the entire island is a museum, and was declared a World Heritage Site in 1991. Over the centuries, political prisoners, common criminals, military deserters, mental patients and even lepers were imprisoned or confined to 'The Island'. The early authorities, and others after them, decided the island made a good prison separated as it is from the mainland by 11km (6,8 miles) of sea, but close enough to Cape Town to be easily supplied with provisions.

The authorities soon realised that it was also an ideal place to keep political leaders banished far away from their people. In addition to Mandela, leaders including Govan Mbeki (President Thabo Mbeki's father), Walter Sisulu and Robert Sobukwe were all imprisoned here.

Conditions on the island were harsh, and many prisoners where forced to do hard labour. Mandela and others were made to work in a lime quarry breaking rocks with hammers, and the dust and bright light reflecting off the white stones caused eye problems for many prisoners. After his release from prison, photographers were asked to be cautious about using flashguns when photographing Mandela because the light hurt his eyes.

In South Africa it is considered a badge of honour to have served prison time for political offences on 'The Island'.

From 1846–1931, the island was also used as a camp for patients suffering from leprosy and mental illnesses. During the Second World War, Robben

Africans visit this as a form of pilgrimage. To them Robben Island is inextricably linked to liberation from apartheid.

Ferries sail daily from the V & A Waterfront jetty, and the entire trip lasts about three hours. The boat trip itself takes about 25 minutes. *Tours: Tel: (021) 419 1300. www.robben-island.org.za. Ferries leave the V & A Waterfront hourly 8am–3pm. Book in advance. Summer sunset tours at 5pm & 6pm. Admission charge.*

Opposite: Tourists on a tour of the prison on Robben Island.
Above: Nelson Mandela's cell in which he spent 18 years
Below: Robben Island in the distance seen from Greenpoint

Island was used as a defence station, and heavy guns were mounted on the island to protect Cape Town harbour.

Since 1997, the entire island has been a museum, and is also used for educational tours and camps for both young people and adults. The island also has a reasonable wildlife population including bontebok, springbok, steenbok and eland. More than 120 species of birds, including ostriches (introduced), and African penguins have been recorded. Southern right whales, dolphins and Cape fur seals are regularly seen in the surrounding waters. Thousands of tourists visit the island every month, often guided by people who were imprisoned on the island themselves.

The focal point of the trip for many is Mandela's small cell, and many South

Nelson Mandela

Nelson Mandela is undoubtedly the most famous South African in history, and for almost 27 years he was, albeit unwillingly, a resident of the Western Cape.

He was imprisoned on Robben Island 11km (7 miles) from Cape Town's beaches from 1964 until 1982. He was then moved to Pollsmoor Prison in Cape Town, and later to Victor Verster Prison near Paarl, from where he was released in February 1990.

Mandela's name is synonymous with that of the freedom struggle in South Africa, and nobody played a greater role in ensuring South Africa's transition to democracy.

'Madiba', as he is known to millions of South Africans, was born in 1918

AP Photo / Themba Hadebe

in the rural Eastern Cape (then called the Transkei). He later became a student at the University of Fort Hare which was reserved for Black students, and it was here that he met Oliver Tambo, later to become president of the ANC, and other politically minded students.

He later completed his law degree at university in Johannesburg, and married Winnie Madikizela in 1958. He practised as a lawyer in Johannesburg, but became increasingly involved in politics, and after the ANC was banned in 1960, he went underground to help form Umkhonto we Sizwe ('the spear of the nation') – the armed wing of the ANC.

Mandela also visited Algeria for military training, and travelled extensively trying to garner support for the ANC. He was arrested in 1962 for having left the country illegally but later, after the police raided a secret ANC house in Rivonia, Johannesburg, the charges were changed to high treason. He and other leaders were sentenced to life imprisonment, and it was during this period that his stature as an icon of the struggle was cemented, both in South Africa and internationally.

After his release in 1990, Mandela was pivotal in ensuring the political negotiations with the National Party Government stayed on track. On several occasions, when political developments threatened the future of negotiations, it was Mandela who managed to calm the emotions of the majority of South Africans. He became president of South Africa in 1994.

In 1996, he divorced Winnie who had become increasingly embroiled in scandals, and two years later married Graca Machel, the widow of former Mozambican President Samora Machel.

Mandela became immensely popular among the vast majority of South Africans of all races due of his integrity and even-handed approach to issues. He stood down in 1999, when Thabo Mbeki became president. He was a favourite with people from all walks of life, even when president, because of his unfailing friendly approach. Thousands of people have heard his friendly "Hello, how are you?" when he stops to chat with everyone from business people to cleaners, from film stars to schoolchildren.

Ironically, given his brutal imprisonment on Robben Island, he now has a home in the exclusive Bishopscourt neighbourhood in Cape Town, and his staff tell the story that soon after Mandela moved in after standing down as

president, he realised that he had run out of sugar. As is befitting with this humble man, he strolled past his sleeping sentry, popped into his neighbour's property and knocked on the back door. "I'm sorry to worry you", he is reported to have said to his neighbour. "I have just moved in next door. My name is Nelson Mandela, and I wonder if I could borrow a cup of sugar?"

Opposite: Nelson Mandela with the 2004 Olympic torch
Below: Nelson Mandela in a serious mood

Photo / Cliff Shain

Walk: Table Mountain

There are hundreds of walks along the slopes of Table Mountain and the nearby mountain chains. Some are easy ambles, and others are tough hikes right to the top of the mountain. Most of the walks are easy to access, and all offer spectacular and different perspectives of Cape Town and surrounding areas. It is best to walk in company for safety reasons. It is also advisable to take a guide if you are planning to go to the top of the mountain.

Cableway view of Table Mountain

View of Camps Bay

1 Platteklip Gorge

This path starts on Tafelberg Road (which runs across the lower slopes of the mountain) about a kilometre past the lower cable station, and heads up the face of the mountain. This is one of the most regularly used routes and is quite easy to follow. The path is very steep and cuts back and forth across the gorge. It usually takes about two hours to get to the top. From the top of the path, it is about a 500-metre walk to the cable station, and an easy ride down the mountain. There is also a restaurant where tired walkers can enjoy well-deserved refreshments and a meal.

2 The Pipe Track

This easy walk starts opposite the parking lot on Kloof Nek road near the lower cable station. The Pipe Track is a lovely contour-path walk which offers great views of Camps Bay, Llandudno, the Twelve Apostles and the coastline. It runs for about 8km (5 miles). For the more adventurous, there are several tracks that lead up Table Mountain from the Pipe Track.

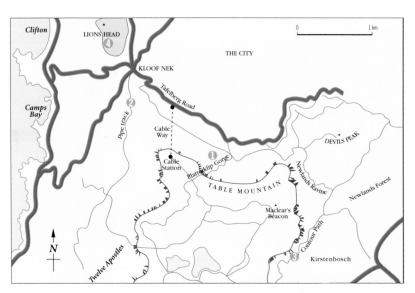

3 The Contour Path

This lovely walk winds its way right across the western face of Table Mountain and usually takes two and a half to three hours one way. It begins near the parking lot close to the corner of Kloof Nek Road and Tafelberg Road. The first part is quite steep, and from the ruins of the Lookout Hut there are good views of Camps Bay, Llandudno and the Twelve Apostles. From here, the path passes under the cable car route to the summit, and continues beneath the rugged face of the famous mountain. The trail continues around Devils Peak and ends at Constantia Nek, although it may be a good idea to be collected at the Rhodes Memorial.

4 Lions Head

This walk provides excellent views of Table Mountain and parts of the city. It begins opposite the parking lot at the top of Kloof Nek Road, and usually takes about an hour to walk along the Signal Hill ridge which leads towards Lions Head.

WALKING TIPS

- If you are planning to hike to the top of Table Mountain, or any other mountain in the area, remember to find out about the weather forecast first. Weather conditions can change very quickly, and mist, rain and high winds sometimes make the mountains extremely unfriendly places.

- Remember to take water and a warm jacket (preferably waterproof) or sweater with you.

- Pick up good maps from one of the tourism offices in Cape Town. There are several good guides to Table Mountain Walks available in bookstores throughout the city.

- Always stick to well-defined routes, and do not leave the path.

The Beaches – Cape Town and the Peninsula

Capetonians are just as proud of 'their' beaches as they are of 'their' mountains. There are some spectacular beaches along this stretch of coast, but take note that the water along the Atlantic seaboard is cold, and sometimes icy. However, the sea along the False Bay coast is usually considerably warmer.

The calm, clear waters of Fish Hoek

The mountains along the coast create small microclimates which means that sometimes the wind may be howling along one bit of the coast, but other beaches elsewhere may be calm.

Speak to the locals who often know the weather secrets of the area, and can suggest the best beach options for the day.

Camps Bay

Llandudno Beach

Bloubergstrand

The view of Table Mountain from Bloubergstrand is one of the most famous in the world and has been photographed millions of times. Many people visit the beach simply to look at the view, but it is also a favourite for lazy days on the sand, picnics or more energetic swimming, windsurfing and other watersports.

Camps Bay

A popular and fashionable beach, and rightly so, because on a good day it makes a spectacular sight with the pale sand offset by the sea, and framed by the Twelve Apostles towering above. In summer, the beach attracts hordes of people, some who come to show off their bodies and get their tan just right so they'll look good in the nearby restaurants and bars in the evening. In the early mornings, evenings and winter, many locals walk their dogs on the beach creating a somewhat more bucolic atmosphere.

Clifton

If anything, the beachgoers at Clifton are even more fashion-conscious than those at Camps Bay. This is model, or model look-alike, sunbathing country. There are four beaches at Clifton, all surrounded by chic apartments and bungalows stacked up the steep slopes overlooking the beaches. There are no shops near the beaches but vendors sell refreshments.

Fish Hoek

This is one of Cape Town's most popular surfing spots, and the relatively calm waters make it a family favourite. The town is fairly sleepy, but the train or road trip from Muizenberg offers good coastal sightseeing.

Muizenberg

Hout Bay

The broad, sandy beach at Hout Bay is very much a family-outing destination. The nearby Mariners' Wharf offers seafood ranging from fish and chips to fresh crayfish and oysters. The water here is also cold, but usually less so than at Clifton.

Kleinmond and Betty's Bay

About 70km (43 miles) from Cape Town, along the dramatic False Bay coast, are Betty's Bay and Kleinmond. Both have good, usually quiet, beaches, with reasonably warm water. Visiting these beaches makes a good day trip from Cape Town.

Kommetjie and Scarborough

These two villages are tiny collections of houses along the Peninsula on the way to Cape Point.

The coastline here is exceptionally scenic, and very popular among surfers due to the assortment of inshore reefs which help to create good waves. The water is cold but invigorating on a hot day.

Llandudno

Hidden away at the foot of the expensive homes of Llandudno, this secluded beach has little of the glamour and glitz of Clifton or Camps Bay, but nevertheless has its own faithful fans. It is a good spot for boardsailing, and in summer, as with Camps Bay, offers lovely views of the setting sun.

Noordhoek

This is a vast 6km (3,7 mile) expanse of white sand that is ideal for leisurely walks and horseback riding. Riding schools in the area exercise their horses on the beach daily, and rides can be arranged. It is a popular surfing beach, but the currents here can be dangerous.

Muizenberg

Popular among surfers and swimmers alike, Muizenberg is warmer than the Atlantic beaches but sometimes quite windy. It is considered to be a fairly safe bathing beach because the water deepens gradually and consistently.

The Cape of Good Hope Nature Reserve

There are good beaches in the reserve, and some offer reasonable snorkelling opportunities. They are often deserted, so be cautious if swimming alone.

Noordhoek Beach

These small black and white birds are Africa's only endemic penguin, and the colony at Boulders Beach near Simon's Town is one of the most popular tourist destinations on the Cape Peninsula.

'Cute' and 'adorable' are two of the most common adjectives used to describe the African penguin, which is about 60cm (2ft) long, and decked out in handsome black and white plumage.

When they waddle along the beach, the stout little birds look anything but elegant, but once they reach the water they are transformed into masters of grace and agility. The birds launch themselves into the water with a comical, but highly effective dive, before heading out to sea.

On their return they 'surf' up to the beach on their tummies before springing up and waddling along with their remnant wings, which they use as fins, spread out for balance. The African penguin makes a noisy braying call, which resulted in it previously being known as the jackass penguin.

Boulders Beach is one of this penguin's few mainland breeding sites, with most birds preferring to use offshore islands up to the Namibian border in the northwest, and all the way around to Bird Island off Port Elizabeth on the east coast.

The penguins nest in burrows, which smell strongly of fish. This is not surprising as their main diet is fish, squid and octopus, which they usually hunt within 10–15km (5,5–10 miles) from shore, and usually within 50km (30 miles) of their home colony.

Juvenile birds often wander much greater distances. Their population has declined steeply over the last 50 years, primarily due to human over-exploitation of the fish stocks, which are their primary food source.

In June 2000 the African penguins of the Western Cape faced an even greater threat when a ship sank near the coast causing widespread oil pollution, but a huge rescue operation, one of the largest of its kind anywhere, saved many of the birds. Some 21,000 oiled penguins were treated. Of these, more than 20,000 birds were taken by road to Port Elizabeth where they were released back into the sea in the hope that the oil would be cleared up by the time they had made the trip home.

Three of the penguins, named Percy, Peter and Pamela, were fitted with satellite tags, and became the subject of dozens of newspaper and television stories around the world as they swam back to their home islands near Cape Town, a distance of some 770km (481 miles).

Peter did the trip to Robben Island in 18 days, and Percy and Pamela made it back to Dassen Island, a further 70km (44 miles) to the north of Cape Town in 15 and 22 days respectively. Most of the birds released at Port Elizabeth made the trip home successfully.

Several other penguin species are occasionally found along South Africa's shores, but these birds have usually been forced north by storms in the vast southern ocean, which reaches all the way to Antarctica.

The African penguin is also found further north along the African West Coast, including Namibia and Angola.

Opposite above: African penguins
Opposite below: Sunbathing on the beach
Above: Coming ashore at Boulders Beach

A seemingly endless variety of flowers, succulents, trees and shrubs adorn the carefully tended gardens and manicured lawns that sweep up towards the steep, forested mountain slopes above.

Kirstenbosch's splendid setting is alone worth the visit, but these gardens, founded in 1913, are also famous among botanists worldwide for the variety of indigenous plants grown here. There are some non-indigenous trees, including oak trees, an almond hedge planted by Jan van Riebeeck in 1660, and some camphor and fig trees planted by Cecil John Rhodes.

There are almost 9,000 species of plants at Kirstenbosch which covers 560 hectares (1,344 acres) of which some 36 hectares (84 acres) are landscaped gardens.

There are several theme gardens which include a peninsular garden featuring plants typical of the Cape Peninsula, a medicinal plants garden, a fragrance garden and several others. The fragrance garden has been designed with sight-impaired visitors in mind by following a braille trail.

The medicinal plant garden is fascinating, and many traditional medicinal plants are carefully labelled with short notes explaining their use. This area is linked to the 'useful plants garden'. Many rare plants of scientific and educational interest grow in the gardens. The gardens have been carefully designed so that irrespective of the season there are always some flowers in bloom.

There are a number of signposted walks ranging from short ambles to a 6km (3,7 miles) trail which meanders through the gardens and along the mountain slopes.

The fit can walk and scramble to the top of Table Mountain via a path, the Smuts Track, which begins at Kirstenbosch. It is best to be prepared for any kind of weather when tackling this challenging trail.

A good way of seeing the gardens is to hire a shuttle-car (golf cart) with a guide. These can be hired at the entrance. Handsets with recorded information about the gardens can be hired by those willing to walk (handsets available 9am–3pm). There are also

guided walks for parties of four or more. Most people simply buy a map, and spend hours wandering around enjoying the gardens and the wonderful views of the eastern side of Table Mountain, False Bay and the Cape Flats.

The climate-controlled conservatory, which alone contains more than 4,000 species of plants, is a 'country under one roof'. It houses plants from all over South Africa which would otherwise not grow in Cape Town's climate. The largest plant in the conservatory is a baobab tree which usually grows in the hot, dry, northern regions of South Africa. The Alpine House contains plants from mountain ranges throughout the country.

Kirstenbosch is also a botanical research centre, with botanists and other scientists conducting research and running education programmes. It has an extensive library of botanical literature, and scientific and popular articles are regularly published.

There is a very good visitors' centre and restaurant, and in summer weekend concerts are held on the lawns. Winter performances take place inside the visitors' centre. Call the information centre for details.
Tel: (021) 762 1166.
www.kirstenbosch.co.za
Open: Apr–Aug 8am–6pm,
Sept–Mar 8am–7pm.
Admission charge.

Opposite: The Kirstenbosch National Botanical Gardens are famous for the large variety of indigenous plant and tree species which have been carefully cultivated
Above: A cool, secluded spot under a fig tree in the gardens

Tour: The Cape Peninsula

The Cape Peninsula's mountain chain curves south from Cape Town, dips at Constantia Nek, rises at the Constantiaberg, falls away over Silvermine to the Fish Hoek Valley, and then swings past Simon's Town to the southeast. For 12km (7,5 miles), before finally tumbling into the sea at Cape Point, it blends into the unspoilt wilderness of the Cape of Good Hope Nature Reserve (now part of the Table Mountain National Park).

Allow one day for this tour. In the centre of Cape Town, take Somerset Road at its junction with Buitengracht Street, and continue along Main Road through Sea Point to the M6.

Vineyards beneath the Constantiaberg mountains

1 The Atlantic Seaboard

Sea Point's promenade is a favourite stretch for slow walks or faster jogs. Further on, at Bantry Bay, little Saunders Rock Beach with its tidal pool offers safe bathing. Beyond, Clifton has the country's most fashionable beaches. Next door, Camps Bay's beaches are

Holiday houses cluster around the secluded beach at Smitswinkelbaai

sprawled dramatically at the foot of the magnificent Twelve Apostles. The road winds on past Bakoven to Llandudno, picturesquely climbing up steep slopes, with Sandy Bay, a nudist beach, beyond.
The M6 climbs the hill above Llandudno, then descends towards Hout Bay.

2 Houtbay

Wood (*hout*) was obtained here for early Cape Town buildings. The town has a lovely beach, a waterfront development and a fishing harbour which is the centre of the snoek industry and the base of the crayfishing fleet. The World of Birds Sanctuary is in the Hout Bay Valley.
Return to the M6, and follow the signs to Chapman's Peak.

3 Chapman's Peak

The 10km (6,2 miles) drive around Chapman's Peak to Noordhoek is one of the world's most spectacular scenic passes, with exceptional views across the bay. It gives access to excellent climbs and mountain walks.
From Noordhoek, follow the M6 from which, after the first lights, the M65 branches right to Kommetjie.

4 Noordhoek and Kommetjie

Noordhoek's lovely 6km (3,7 miles) Long Beach is favoured by horseback riders. At its end, Kommetjie is a quiet village with a popular surfing beach. A shallow tidal pool provides safe bathing for children.
From Kommetjie, the M65 continues through Scarborough to the Cape of Good Hope.

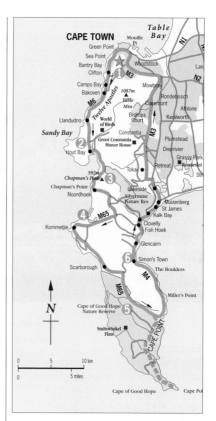

Camps Bay beneath Lions Head

Copyright: South African Tourism

A spectacular aerial view of Cape Point

5 Cape of Good Hope

This magnificent 7,750-hectare nature reserve (mountain zebra, bontebok, eland, baboons) straddles the peninsula's tip, and is now included in the Table Mountain National Park. There are drives, and places to picnic and swim.

The view from Cape Point across False Bay, so called because it was often mistaken for Table Bay, is spectacular.

At the exit, turn right if you want to visit the southern tip, then return north, turning right onto the M4 to Simon's Town.

6 False Bay

After passing Smitswinkelbaai, the approach to Simon's Town is via

The Boulders, where the swimming, among huge boulders, is shared with a colony of African penguins. Simon's

An important colony of African penguins nest at the protected Boulders beach

Town, South Africa's largest naval base, is a quaint seaside town, beyond which Fishhoek is a popular resort with wide, safe beaches. Kalk Bay, with antique, junk and craft shops, is home to the False Bay fishing fleet. Beyond, St James has a small beach with a tidal pool. Alongside it, Muizenberg's magnificent beach offers safe bathing.

Visit the **Natale Labia Museum** and **Rhodes Cottage Memorial Museum**. *Continue on the M4 past Lakeside, and follow the signs to the M3 and the city.*

Cape of Good Hope
Tel: (021) 701 8692.
www.tmnp.co.za
Open: daily.
Admission charge.

Fishing boats in Kalk Bay harbour

Simon's Town is South Africa's oldest naval base

Simon's Town Museum
Court Rd, Simon's Town.
Tel: (021) 786 3046.
Open: Tues–Fri 10am–4pm,
Sat 11am–4pm.
Closed: Sun, Christmas Day & Good Friday.
Admission charge.

Natale Labia Museum
192 Main Rd, Muizenberg.
Tel: (021) 788 4106.
Open: Mon–Sat 10am–5pm.
Admission charge.

Rhodes Cottage
Main Rd, Muizenberg.
Tel (021) 788 1816.
Open: 9am–4pm.
Donation.

Common Mammals of the Western Cape

Cape Fur Seals

Cape fur seals are often seen in the port near the V & A Waterfront and in Kalk Bay harbour. The males are much larger than the females, and sometimes weigh more than 300kg (660lb), and reach lengths of 2,2m (7ft 2in). Females usually weigh between 40–80kg (88–176lb), and seldom grow longer than 1,4m (4ft 7in).

The Cape fur seal is primarily a fish-eater, but pups sometimes eat rock lobsters. Some fishermen accuse seals of stealing a large proportion of their catch, but this claim is disputed by scientists.

Bontebok

This remarkably handsome antelope, which is endemic to the Western Cape, used to occur here in large numbers but was hunted almost to the point of extinction in the 19th century. Although the population has recovered through careful conservation programmes, it is still one of the rarest antelope in South Africa. The male is particularly striking with its black and brown coat contrasting sharply with its white blaze, belly and rump. Bontebok are exclusively grazers, and can easily be spotted on the grassy plains of the Bontebok National Park (near Swellendam), the Cape of Good Hope Nature Reserve and in De Hoop Nature Reserve (near Cape Agulhas).

Klipspringer

Steep, rocky mountain slopes are the preferred habitat of this remarkable little antelope which occurs throughout the Western Cape. Klipspringers have specially adapted pointed hooves which enable them to get a grip on smooth rock surfaces and climb to places inaccessible to predators. They form permanent pairs, with both sexes defending their territory.

When klipspringers feel threatened, they run a short distance, and then stop and look back at the danger, confident that they can flee up steep rock faces if necessary. Klipspringers stand about 0,5m (1ft 8in) at the shoulder. They eat a variety of shrubs and herbs, and do not need to drink water regularly.

Springbok

South Africa's national animal prefers the drier central and western regions of the

Copyright: South African Tourism

Opposite left: Cape fur seals resting on the rocks
Opposite right: Springbok are South Africa's national animal
Left: Bontebok are endemic to the Western Cape
Below: A rock dassie sunbathing

country, and used to form herds hundreds of thousands strong as they migrated in search of fresh grazing. Today their population is much smaller, but springbok are common enough in game reserves and on many farms. They are medium-sized antelope, standing about 0,75m (2ft 6in) at the shoulder. Springbok sometimes pronk (they jump high into the air with head down and back arched). This is believed to be in response to predators, the theory being that the animal that jumps the highest is the strongest and most difficult to catch.

Steenbok

These tiny antelope are common in many parts of South Africa, and are often seen in the same area because they form territories which they defend against other steenbok. They only weigh about 11kg (24lb), and have very appealing 'Bambi' faces, framed by large, delicate ears. They are particularly common in the Karoo. Steenbok have a unique gland underneath their jaw which they use to scent-mark their territories.

ROCK DASSIES

These curious little creatures are often seen on rocky mountain slopes in the Cape, and are common on Table Mountain near the cable station. Dassies, members of the hyrax family, are often mistakenly referred to as rock rabbits, but they are not a related species. Oddly enough they share certain genetic characteristics and other biological similarities with elephants.

The rock dassie lives in colonies, and often spends time in the morning lazing in the sun and warming up before heading off to feed. They are the primary prey species of the black eagle. In some areas, particularly on Table Mountain, dassies have been dying because they eat discarded cigarette ends.

Some remarkable birds are found in the Western Cape, and although there are not as many species that occur as in the Kruger National Park or KwaZulu-Natal, they are no less interesting. Some species, including protea canary, orange-breasted sunbird and Cape sugarbird occur nowhere else, and they are well adapted to life in the *fynbos*. Seabirds, occurring only in the vast southern oceans, are also occasionally blown inshore by winter storms – a treat for birdwatchers, if not the tired birds.

Copyright: South African Tourism

Black Eagles

The large spectacular eagles are birds of the mountains, and are often seen soaring gracefully on thermals close to Table Mountain. Each pair of eagles closely guard their territory against intruders, and often perform spectacular aerial displays intended to ward intruders off. They use the same nesting site on a cliff or mountainside for years, adding more sticks to the already large messy nests whenever they feel it necessary. Rock dassies form the bulk of their diet, but they will kill other small mammals if given the opportunity.

Blue Crane

South Africa's national bird, the blue crane, is a tall, stately bird standing over a metre (3ft 3in) tall. They are quite common, and are often seen feeding in the wheatfields of the Western Cape. They eat a variety of seeds, grains, bulbs and plant foliage, as well as insects, frogs and small mammals. Crowned cranes sometimes hold their wings open, and kick their legs up in a strange dance before breeding.

Cape Gannet

These large seabirds are common around Cape Town, and the sight of a flock diving into the sea after fish is a memorable sight. The birds fold their wings back, and plummet into the sea from a height of 20–30m (6,5–9,8ft), the entire flock diving in a frenzy of action and splashes. Gannets breed on islands along the coast, and form dense, noisy colonies. Their droppings, harvested in the form of guano, which is used as fertiliser, form a thick coating on the islands.

Orange-breasted Sunbird

Although these small birds do not match any of the others listed here in size, the males resemble flying jewels of brilliant colour. They are endemic to the fynbos of the Western Cape, and can be seen on the slopes of Table Mountain and elsewhere throughout the Peninsula. They feed on nectar and insects which they catch on the wing. The female, as with all species of sunbirds, is much duller than the male. Catching a glimpse

Copyright: South African Tourism

popular tourist attraction in the Western Cape and Little Karoo.

Originally bred domestically for their feathers which were used as fashion items, they are today used to stage races, complete with jockeys. They are also bred for their meat and skin which is used to make leather.

Ostriches weigh from 60–80kg (132–176lb), but exceptional birds weighing well over 100kg (220lb) have been recorded.

The male has black body feathers with white tips on its wings, while the females are a greyish-brown.

of the male with his iridescent green head and bright orange breast is sure to thrill even non-birdwatchers.

Ostrich

The world's largest living bird, sometimes standing two metres (6ft 6in) tall, is a

Opposite: Black eagles only occur in mountainous regions
Top: Orange-breasted sunbirds are common in the *fynbos*
Below: Ostrich-farming in the Western Cape

Copyright: South African Tourism

Tour: West Coast

Although this region lacks the glamour of the winelands and the Garden Route, the West Coast makes an interesting day trip from Cape Town.

Allow a day, or two days if you intend spending the night in the West Coast National Park or Darling. Leave Cape Town on the N1, and then take the R27/Milnerton Road.

Capetonian with his catch-of-the-day

The West Coast is very much a fishing region, and the nutrient-rich waters of the cold Benguela Current yield a handsome harvest of mackerel, sardines, pilchards and other pelagic species. The coast is also well known for its spring flowers which, although not as vivid as those in Namaqualand further north, are still impressive. The best time to visit is August or September when the flowers blossom.

1 Bloubergstrand

It is worth stopping here to enjoy the famous view of Table Mountain across Table Bay. The best view is from the beach. If the weather is clear, you will be able to shoot exactly the same photograph that has graced thousands of postcards and calendars.

Proceed north until you reach the Darling turnoff to your right. Take the R315.

Darling is a growing tourism attraction, and has several comfortable B&Bs and restaurants

Tienie Versveld Flower Reserve

(this is on the right next to the road)
The wild flowers usually bloom
around August or September after
late winter rains, but is it worth
asking the Darling tourism where
the flowers are best.
*Proceed to Darling a few kilometres
further east.*

2 Darling

Pieter Dirk-Uys, one of South
Africa's foremost satirists, has
bought and renovated the old
Darling Station, and turned it into
a theatre and restaurant called
Evita se Perron. Dirk-Uys is
famous as Evita Bezuidenhout,
his fictitious alter-ego who
comments on all aspects of
South African society.

There are performances on most
Fridays, Saturdays and Sundays.
Call to confirm shows and times.
It also has a small museum with all
the usual memorabilia and displays
explaining the history of the region.
If you intend going to an evening
theatre performance, stay in the
town for the night. There are
several wine cellars in the area,
and every September the town
hosts a flower show, the highlight
of the year.

Evita se Perron
Arcadia St, Darling.
Tel: (022) 492 2851.
www.evita.co.za

Butter Museum
Pastorie St, Darling.
Tel: (022) 492 3361.

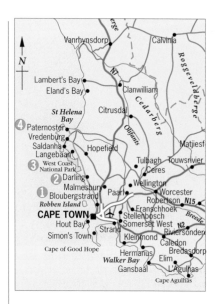

Paternoster fishing boats

The West Coast National Park and the Langebaan Lagoon protect a diverse array of habitats as well as birds, flowers and animals

Darling Tourism
Tel: (022) 492 3361.
www.darlingtourism.co.za
Open: daily 10am–1pm & 2–4pm.

Retrace your route along the R315, and then head north on the R27 to the West Coast National Park.

3 West Coast National Park
As with the other parks in the area, the best time to visit is when the flowers are in bloom, but there are also lovely views along the coast. The wetlands here are globally important, and waders from as far away as Siberia migrate here every summer.

The Langebaan Lagoon forms the focal point of the park. Allow quite a bit of time for driving through the park.
Central Reservations.
Tel: (012) 428 9111.
www.parks-sa.co.za

Continue north on the R27, and follow the signs to Paternoster along the R399, bypassing the town of Vredenberg.

4 Paternoster
The small, whitewashed fisherman's cottages are favourites among photographers in this village where life revolves around the fishing industry, and, in recent years, tourism.

There are several good seafood restaurants in the village. The nearby Cape Columbine Nature Reserve is another good flower area.
From Paternoster, return along the R399 until it becomes the R45, and follow this road for 84km (51 miles) until it joins the N7 to Cape Town. It is another 70km (43,5 miles) to central Cape Town, less than an hour's drive.

The *Evita se Perron* theatre is housed in the old Darling train station

Flowers

The mountains and beaches of the Cape are remarkably beautiful, but it is the variety of flora that really demand superlatives. The Cape Floral Kingdom, with more than 7,700 species, is the richest on Earth, although it is also the smallest botanical kingdom.

The Cape Peninsula alone has more plant species than Britain. South Africa as a whole supports more than 22,000 species, 10 per cent of the global plant diversity. (The other plant kingdoms which cover the entire surface of the Earth are the Paleotropical, Neotropical, Holarctic, Australian and Holantarctic).

The Cape Floral kingdom stretches from Cape Town to Port Elizabeth, 760km (475 miles) east, and then northwards from Cape Town for about 350km (218 miles) to Nieuwoudtville.

The dominant species throughout the region is the *fynbos* (meaning 'fine bush', but more accurately referring to the fine leaves of the plants). The plants are adapted to the nutrient-poor soils of the region, the dry summers and regular fires.

The most obvious species within the *fynbos* are the proteas which are well known in flower arrangements throughout the world. The protea is also South Africa's national flower.

Proteas are pollinated by a fascinating variety of creatures including mice, gerbils, birds and beetles all of which are attracted by the sweet syrup the flowers exude. Some seeds are dispersed by wind and others by ants.

Other species which make up *fynbos* are ericas, orchids, restios (various forms of reeds) and a range of heaths. One of the prettiest flowers is the red disa, commonly known as the 'pride of Table Mountain'.

Other Cape plants that are well-known globally are the geraniums (pelargoniums), watsonias, agapanthus and irises which were taken to Europe by early settlers.

The Cape's fold mountains and valleys help create a wide variety of 'microclimates', some which support flowers that grow nowhere else. This makes many plants extremely vulnerable to extinction because a single poorly planned commercial farm or property-development can wipe out an entire population of plants.

The largest family group of flowers are the daisies of which there are more than 1,000 species, most of which are endemic. Many of these grow on the West Coast and further north in Namaqualand. Brightly coloured '*vygies*' (mesembryanthemums), while not really part of the *fynbos*, grow in profusion along the West Coast.

There is also a large number of bulbous plants. The bulbs are a useful defence against fire, because even if the leaves are destroyed, the plant can grow again from the bulb which has been protected by the soil.

The biggest threats to the *fynbos* are both human development and alien-invader species.

As noted earlier, human development removes large areas of indigenous plant life – grape vines have accounted for thousands of hectares of *fynbos* being removed, which is devastating not only for the plants but the many species of mammals, birds, reptiles and insects which are dependent on *fynbos*.

Alien plant species including the Port Jackson pine, Australian wattle and other commercial forests (predominantly pine and eucalyptus trees) have destroyed tens of thousands of hectares of *fynbos*.

Opposite: Fynbos is the predominant vegetation throughout the Western Cape
Above: Protea – one of the most spectacular species among the *fynbos*

Tour: False Bay Coast and Hermanus

This trip takes in some of the best the Cape has to offer: wine estates, lovely mountain and sea views, penguins and, in the right season, whales. All along the way there are lovely beaches, nature reserves, restaurants and then some more mountain and sea vistas.

This tour can be done in a day, but it is a far better idea to spend one or two nights in the Hermanus area, particularly during whale season. Leave Cape Town on the N2 national road and head to Somerset West. Take the R44/Broadway offramp and follow the signs to Vergelegen.

Perlemoen (abalone) are an expensive seafood delicacy, and the shells are sold as souvenirs

1 Vergelegen

The classic Cape Dutch architecture, row upon row of grape vines and the backdrop of the Hottentots Holland mountains, make Vergelegen a lovely place to visit. Founded in 1817, it is one of the most successful estates in the Cape.

Nearby is the **Helderberg Nature Reserve** which has lovely walks of varying length along the fynbos-covered slopes of the Helderberg mountains. If you have time, these walks provide rewarding views of False Bay and the various mountain ranges. It is also a good opportunity to learn about the *fynbos* and the birds and other creatures that live there.

From Somerset West take the R44 to Gordon's Bay, and then all the way round the coast until it joins the R43.

2 Gordon's Bay

Gordon's Bay is a small town with good swimming, some restaurants and a busy fishing harbour. From Gordon's Bay the road winds its way along the foot of the mountains just above the sea, and during whale season the huge mammals are commonly spotted all along this coast. Dolphins can also be seen at any time of the year.

Vergelegen is considered by many to be one of the finest examples of Cape Dutch architecture

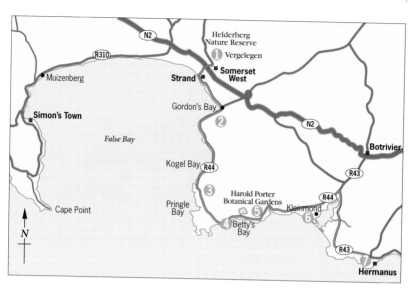

3 Kogel Bay and Pringle Bay

Kogel Bay has a lovely beach, and a few kilometres on is the holiday village of Pringle Bay which shelters beneath the peak of Cape Hangklip. Cape Point is usually visible across False Bay to the west.

4 Betty's Bay

A quiet holiday village with a pleasant beach. Look for the signs that point the way to the penguin colony at Stony Point. This is only one of three African penguin colonies on the mainland.

5 Harold Porter Botanical Gardens

The gardens are about two kilometres from Betty's Bay, the entrance is just off the road. The gardens are an excellent example of the vegetation of the area. There is a very short walk, about 10 minutes, to a waterfall a little way up the ravine.

6 Kleinmond

This small holiday town is at the mouth of the Bot River. There is good beach here that is ideal for walking. The Kleinmond Coastal and Mountain Nature Reserve is just outside the town.
After 12km join the R43, and turn right to Hermanus.

7 Hermanus

Traditionally a seaside holiday town with lovely scenery, Hermanus is now the centre of a vibrant whale-watching industry.

There are good places to stay, and lots of restaurants. The main shopping area is small and easy to walk around.
Return to the N2 via the R43, and then drive over the scenic Sir Lowry's Pass back to Cape Town.

Southern right whales swim so close inshore along the Cape Coast it sometimes seems that they have come to watch people, rather than the other way round.

Every year, usually between June and November, the whales migrate to the warm coastal waters to mate and give birth. In keeping with tourism trends worldwide, a thriving whale-watching industry has grown along the coast to take advantage of this phenomenon.

Humpback whales are also spotted regularly along the coast, particularly closer to KwaZulu-Natal, as they migrate towards their breeding-grounds near Madagascar.

Many other species of whales have been recorded in South African waters, but they are usually temporary visitors, preferring to spend most of their lives far from land.

These include the blue whale, the world's largest creature (the heaviest recorded one weighed 9,300kg/93 tons),

killer whales and 21 other whale species, some of which are very poorly known to science.

The Cape coast is also an excellent place to watch some of the 12 dolphin species that occur in South African waters. The most commonly seen species are the Heaviside's, bottlenose, dusky and common dolphins.

Much of the whale-watching industry is centred around the southern right whale, which reaches 17m (58ft) in length. Their calves already measure 5–6m (16–20ft) at birth.

They spend most of the year in the cold, nutrient-rich waters of the southern ocean, but in breeding season large numbers of these whales usually congregate between Cape Point and Plettenberg Bay. Hermanus has become one of the best-known spots to see the whales because the cliffs near the town provide an excellent vantage point to watch them 'breaching' – lifting most of their bodies out of the water, before crashing in again with a huge splash.

They also 'sail' with their heads underwater and their tail flukes protruding into the air.

Often the huge creatures and their calves simply swim along slowly, spending hours close inshore, unknowingly creating excitement for tourists and locals alike.

Although Hermanus prides itself as one of the best places to watch whales, they can be spotted anywhere along the southern Cape coast.

Accordingly there are a good number of companies that specialise in running both land- and boat-based whale watching tours. The boats are strictly regulated, and it is illegal to approach the whales too closely. The area is busy during whale-watching season.

Southern Right Whales

The southern right whale grows to a maximum length of 15–17m (49–56ft) and weighs 50–65 tons (5,000–6,500kg). They are not deep divers, and seldom stay submerged for than 20 minutes. They eat small crustaceans (krill) found relatively close to the surface. Little is known of their social structure, but the mothers form very strong bonds with their calves.

Humpback Whales

These whales grow to about 14m (44ft) in length, and feed on small crustaceans (krill) and small fish. They weigh from

Copyright: South African Tourism

25,000–40,000kg (25–40 tons).

Humpback whales are well known for their 'songs', a series of squeaks, moans and whistles of varying pitch, which can last up to 30 minutes. They usually stay submerged for a fairly short time, and seldom longer than 15 minutes.

Opposite: Southern right whale near Hermanus
Above: Tourists watching a whale on the southern Cape coast

THE WHALE CRIER

Every whale season between June and November, the Hermanus 'whale crier' patrols along the cliffs blowing his kelp horn whenever whales are spotted. He has different codes for each spot on the coast, and his bugle call alerts locals appropriately. Pamphlets explaining the codes are widely distributed in Hermanus and at the tourism bureau. The 'whale crier' can also be contacted on his 'hotline' 083 212 1074.

Stellenbosch Sights

The town, its culture and its economy revolve around the wine industry and the University of Stellenbosch. Many restaurants and pubs rely on students for business, and during term the town bustles with young people. The tourism bureau conducts regular historical walking tours through the town.

The view of Stellenbosch and surrounding vineyards

Be sure to visit the Stellenbosch University Museum which incorporates the Sasol Art Gallery. The museum has collections of everything from art to archaeological artefacts, and the gallery hosts contemporary art exhibitions.

The nearby mountains also offer excellent hiking and walks. The Jonkershoek and Assegaaibosch Nature Reserves have a network of trails which range from short, easy walks to longer hikes.

There is also a Vineyard Hiking Trail that meanders through the mountains for 23km (14 miles). Contact the Tourism Bureau for details.

Burgerhuis, Stellenbosch

Mountain biking and horse riding trips through the area can also be arranged. There are three golf courses within easy reach of the town. Also visit the Stellenryk Wine Museum.

Botanical Gardens
These gardens contain indigenous and exotic plants from all over the world. They are South Africa's oldest university gardens.
Tel: (021) 808 3054.
Open: Mon–Fri 9am–4.30pm,
Sat 9–11am. Call to book for groups,
conducted tours and lectures.
Stellenbosch Tourism Bureau
Tel: (021) 883 3584.
www.stellenbosch.org.za

Burgerhuis
Corner Alex St and Bloem St,
Die Braak.
Tel: (021) 887 0339.
www.museums.co.za
Open: Mon–Fri 8am–4.30pm, Sat
10am–1pm & 2–5pm.
Closed: Sun.
Free admission.

Jonkershoek Nature Reserve
Tel: (021) 866 1560.
Open: Mon–Sun 8am–6pm.

Moederkerk
Drostdy St. Tel: (021) 883 3458.
www.moederkerk.co.za
Open: Mon–Sat, Sun services 9am & 7pm.

Stellenbosch University Museum and Sasol Art Gallery
52 Van Ryneveld St.
Tel: (021) 808 3693.

Stellenryk Wine Museum
Corner Dorp St. and Ann die Waagen St.
Tel: (021) 887 3480.
Open: Mon–Fri 9am–12.45pm & 2–5pm.
Sat 10am–1pm & 2–5pm.
Closed: Sun.

The Village Museum
18 Van Ryneveld St.
Tel: (021) 887 2902.
www.museums.org.za
Open: Mon–Sat 9am–5pm,
Sun 2–5pm.
Closed: Christmas Day and
Good Friday.
Admission charge.

Toy and Miniature Museum
Corner Market St and Herte St.
Tel: (021) 887 2948.
Open: Mon–Sat 9.30am–5pm.
Sun 2–5pm. Closed: May–Aug.
Admission charge.

VOC Kruithuis (Arsenal)
Bloem St, Die Braak.
Open: Mon–Fri 9am–2pm.
Closed: Jun–Aug.

UNIVERSITY SPORT

The Maties vs the Ikeys is a hotly contested rugby match that raises passions and usually ends in raucous parties. The Maties are the powerful, traditionally Afrikaans-speaking University of Stellenbosch rugby team, and the Ikeys are their counterparts from the traditionally English-speaking University of Cape Town.

The rugby match has been a regular fixture of the sporting and social scene of the Western Cape for decades, and some students would rather miss their exams than the game.

Tourists at the VOC Kruithuis (Arsenal)

Walk: Stellenbosch

Stellenbosch has a particular charm partly derived from its oak-lined streets and whitewashed Cape Dutch houses, and the fact that it is also a university town with a fun and laid-back atmosphere. It is perhaps the town most often associated with South African wine, and was founded by Dutch governor Simon van der Stel in 1679. Some streets still have open water canals running down the sides, and many of the old buildings have been beautifully restored. There are numerous fine examples of Cape Dutch architecture. *A tour to Stellenbosch from Cape Town can easily be completed in a day. For those particularly interested in wines, it is worth allowing more time in the area. Park in The Avenues Road, and start at the Moederkerk near the intersection of Drosty and Church streets.*

A curious cat explores the flowers outside Die Burgerhuis national monument, built in 1797

1 Moederkerk

The original church burnt down in 1710 and was replaced with another in 1723. The Moederkerk (Mother Church), as it stands today, was rebuilt in 1863 in the Neo-Gothic style.
Diagonally across the road at 37 Van Ryneveld Street is The Village Museum.

2 The Village Museum

This entire block consists of restored and furnished historic homesteads and gardens from the early-17th to mid-19th century. They are the old Schreuderhuis cottage (1709), the Cape Dutch Bittermanshuis (1789), the Georgian Grosvenor House (1803) and the Victorian Murray House (1850).
Continue west down Plein Street towards The Braak, an open stretch of lawn bounded by many historic buildings.

3 St Mary's on the Braak

This church is on the northern end of the square to your right. It was completed in 1852 and is constructed in Neo-Gothic style. On the western side of the grass square is the Burgerhuis (Citizens House). Burgerhuis was built in 1797 and is now a museum with displays of furniture and other exhibits.
On leaving the Burgerhuis, turn right and pass the VOC Kruithuis.

Stellenbosch slave bells

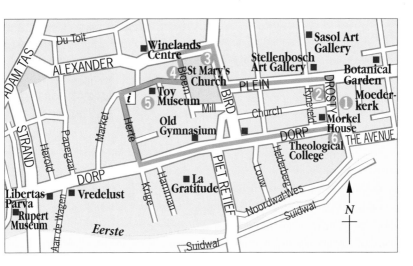

4 VOC Kruithuis (Arsenal)

Built in 1777 by the Dutch East India Company, this is the oldest surviving gun-powder magazine in southern Africa.

Turn into Market Street and continue past the Stellenbosch Publicity Association until you reach the Toy and Miniature Museum.

5 Toy and Miniature Museum

This museum is housed in the old Rheinish Church which was built in 1832. There are dozens of displays of toys, miniature railways and other bits and pieces.

Continue down Market Street and turn right into Dorp Street. Walk all the way back towards The Avenues Road where you parked. Look out for the Theological College on your right.

6 Theological College

This is the site where the Cape Colony Governor Simon van der Stel pitched his

tents in 1679. A church was built on this site in 1687 but it was destroyed by fire in 1710. A new building also fell victim to fire in 1762. The college was erected on the site in 1905.

St Mary's on the Braak Church, built in 1852

Franschhoek

The beautiful Franschhoek Valley is one of South Africa's premier wine-producing areas, and has become an extremely fashionable place to live and to holiday. The town has energetically promoted itself as a tourism attraction and emphasises its historical links to France at every opportunity.

Debonair wine estate Franschhoek

The valley is exceedingly attractive, and there are a variety of excellent restaurants both in the town and at the many wine estates scattered throughout the valley. It is one of the oldest farming regions in South Africa.

In 1688, the Cape Governor Simon van der Stel granted French Huguenot refugees land in the valley which earned the area its name meaning 'French Corner'. The Huguenots were French Protestants who fled their homeland fearing religious persecution.

Grape vines growing in the beautiful Franschhoek Valley

Franshhoek is small town and easy to walk around. There are many restaurants, art galleries and craft shops scattered along the main road and side streets. Many of the wine estates in the valley, some of the best in the Cape, offer wine tasting tours and excellent Cape cooking. Most have stores on the property where wine and sometimes cheese and other products are on sale. In summer, music is played in the gardens at some estates, and others arrange jazz or other recitals in the cellars from time to time.

The valley is surrounded by no fewer than four mountain ranges: The Wemmershoek and Franschhoek mountains to the east and north, and the Klein (small) and Groot (big) Drakenstein mountains to the west and south.

There are a wide variety of walks and hikes in and near the town, and several farms in the valley have trout in their streams and dams, and are happy to hire out fishing equipment. Every July the town hosts the Fly Fishing Festival which coincides with Bastille Day in France. Mountain bike riding and horseback rides through the valley can also be arranged.

The Huguenot Memorial Museum and the tall three-arched Huguenot

Monument are situated in the park close to the town centre. The museum is housed in a replica 18th century house, and contains genealogical records of the early Huguenots and displays of furniture and other items. There is also a small display of South African War memorabilia and a section on national history housed in a building nearby.

Franschhoek makes an easy day-trip from Cape Town, but it is well worth spending a night in the area so you can enjoy the scenery, food and wine to the fullest.

Franschhoek Vale'e Tourisme
Tel: (021) 876 3606.
www.franschhoek.org.za

Dewdale Trout Farm and Fly Fishery
Rent a rod, and, even if you don't catch a trout, enjoy the scenery and head off for a glass of wine.
Dewdale Farm, Robertsvlei.
Tel: (021) 876 2755.
www.dewdale.com

Huguenot Memorial Museum
The museum tells the story of the French Huguenots. There are also displays of Cape Dutch furniture and other items.
Corner Huguenot St and Lambrechts St.
Tel: (021) 876 2532.
Open: Mon–Sat 9am–5pm.
Sun 2–5pm.
www.museums.org.za

CHEESE AND OLIVES

Farmers in the winelands have not only concentrated on grapes and wine. Many manufacture delicious cheese, and others produce high quality olives. Many of the cheeses are modelled on those of Europe, and camembert, pecorino, mozzarella and gorgonzola are displayed next to South African cheeses. Local favourites include cheese flavoured with Madagascar green peppercorns and sweet pepperdews (a mild pepper unique to South Africa). It's fun to make up a picnic of local cheese, olives and wine to enjoy at a quiet spot in the mountains or on a beach. (Remember the sea is only about half an hour away from Stellenbosch or Franschhoek).

Rickety Bridge is one of the newer wine estates in the Franschhoek Valley

The Wine Industry

The South African wine industry has grown by leaps and bounds in recent years, and has developed a considerable export market. There are hundreds of small boutique vineyards scattered throughout the Western Cape, cheekily rubbing shoulders with the big well-established vineyards.

Franschhoek, Stellenbosh, Wellington and Paarl are the best known and most fashionable South African wine-producing regions, but clever winemakers in towns like Worcester, Robertson and Montagu, some 180km (110 miles) from Cape Town, have now leapt into the market.

South Africa has more than 100,000 hectares planted to grapes, and the industry employs about 350,000 people.

Wealthy business people and foreigners, who vie with each other to hire the best and most innovative winemakers, have bought numerous vineyards.

Wine-making and fruit-growing provide economic sustenance for entire valleys in the Western Cape, and even people not directly involved in the cellars earn their livelihoods from associated businesses like restaurants, craft shops, cheese-making and tourism.

Many vineyards offer wine-tasting tours, and others run good restaurants on their properties too. Each region, all in all there are 17 recognised wine routes, offers organised tours, although many tourists opt to drive themselves and spend a few days in the scenic winelands.

Whitewashed, gabled houses surrounded by vines sheltering in valleys beneath high fold mountains make for picturesque touring conditions ideal for enjoying good wine and food. All the regions offer other activities, including horse riding and hiking, and trout, yellowfish and bass fishing. There are a wide range of B&Bs, guest farms and lodges throughout the winelands.

Although experts consider South African red wines to be superior to the whites, many new winemaking techniques and cultivars have been developed to make the most of local conditions. Cabernet Sauvignon, Pinotage and Merlot are the most common red varietals, and they are being planted in increasing quantities, although the local Pinotage cultivars are also popular. There has been a move away from tannin-rich wine to softer fruiter tastes.

Copyright: South African Tourism

There is also a large range of whites with Chardonnay and Sauvignon Blanc being the choice of many growers.

South Africa's winemaking history dates back some 350 years, and the first vineyards were planted in 1655. The industry only really began developing after the arrival of the French Huguenot settlers who had winemaking experience.

South Africa also makes excellent sherry and fortified wines (better known as Port), although European Union trade regulations forbid the use of the more familiar name. Some vineyards can trace their origins back to the arrival of the French Huguenots in the 17th century.

Brandy is also produced in some areas, and there is even a brandy-tasting route.

In recent years, the industry has also made some progress towards being more representative of South Africa's population, and a number of empowerment projects have been developed. Various organisations and farmers have helped former workers raise capital, and in a few cases assisted them in creating their own companies. Education programmes have also been set up.

It is well worth buying one of the many wine guides on offer. The best is John Platter's *Guide to the Wines of South Africa*.

A basic wine guide

There are three production systems under which wine is made and sold in South Africa.

Estate Wines

Estates make wine only from the grapes they themselves grow.

Co-ops (Co-operatives)

Co-ops make wine from the grapes grown by their members. Co-ops make most of South Africa's wine. Members often have access to equipment that is sometimes jointly owned, and to advice from co-op staff.

Cellars

Cellars usually buy grapes (and wine), and make wine that is sold under brand names. Some also add their own grapes to the final product. Some commercial wholesalers also buy wine or grapes in bulk.

Opposite: Bringing in the grape harvest
Above: Wine tasting is offered at many wine estates

South Africa's winelands are divided into official wine of origin regions, but for the purpose of this guide, a few good vineyards of some of the better-known areas (not necessarily according to the official regions) are listed.

There are many other excellent vineyards. Contact the relevant wine route or tourism offices for complete lists.

Constantia (Cape Town)

Buitenverwagting, Constantia Uitsig, Groot Constantia, Klein Constantia and Steenberg vineyards.

Constantia Wine Route
Tel: (021) 788 6193.
Fax: (021) 788 6208.
www.constantiawineroute.co.za

Durbanville (Cape Town)

Altydgedacht, Bloemendal, Durbanville Hills, Meerendal and Nitida.
Durbanville Wine Route
Tel: (021) 558 1300.

Franschhoek

Boschendal, Cabriere Estate, L'Ormarins, La Motte and Rickety Bridge.
Franschhoek Wine Route
Tel: (021) 876 3062.
www.franschhoekwines.co.za

Helderberg

(in and near Somerset West)
Avontuur, Longridge, Meerlust, Vergelegen and Yonder Hill.
Helderberg Wine Route
Tel: (021) 855 2004.
Fax: (021) 855 4083.
hwr@mweb.co.za

Olifants River

Cederberg Cellars and Klawer Winery.
Olifants River Wine Route
Tel: (021) 213 3126.
olifantsrivwineroute@kingsley.co.za

Paarl

Hosts the prestigious Nederberg Wine Auction every year.
Backsberg, Fairview, Laborie, Nederberg and Simonsvlei.
Red Route (Paarl Vintners)
Tel: (021) 872 3841.
paarl@wine.co.za

Robertson

De Wetshof Estate, Graham Beck and Robertson Winery.
Robertson Wine Valley
Tel: (023) 626 1054.
info@robertsonwinevalley.co.za

Stellenbosch
Blaauwklippen, Delaire, Lanzerac,
Rustenburg and Spier.
Stellenbosch Wine Route
Tel: (021) 886 4310.
info@wineroute.co.za

Swartland
Allesverloren, Darling Cellars,
Groote Post, Ormonde and
Swartland Wine Cellar.
Swartland Wine Route
Tel: (022) 487 2063.
www.swartlandwineroute.co.za

Tulbagh
Theuniskraal, Twee Jonge Gazzelen
and Tulbagh Winery.
Tulbagh Wine Route
Tel: (023) 230 1348.
www.tulbaghwineroute.co.za

Wellington
Onverwacht Wine Estate and Wamaker's
Vallei.
Wellington Wine Route
Tel: (021) 873 4604.
www.visitwellington.co.za

Walker Bay
Bouchard Finlayson, Hamilton Russel,
Paul Cluver and Southern Right.

For further information about South
African wine and vineyards, go to
www.winemag.co.za or read Wine
Magazine which is available in South
African book stores.
Wine magazine
Tel: (021) 530 3100.

Opposite: Padagang wine shop near Tulbagh
Below: Autumn colours in the vineyards and
fruit orchards of the Hex River Valley, 140km
(87 miles) from Cape Town

Paarl

Paarl (The Pearl) is another important wine-growing centre, and although it does not share the charm of Stellenbosch or Franschhoek, the wines are no less delicious. Even though the town was established in the early 18th century, the area had been settled and farmed since the late 1600s. Paarl is situated 61km (38 miles) from Cape Town.

Vineyards in Paarl

Prior to the arrival of Dutch settlers, the area was visited regularly by Khoikhoi people of the Chochoque clan who grazed their cattle in the valleys in the area. As more settlers arrived, the Chochoque were gradually forced out of the area, but many worked on the farms that developed.

Although the early Dutch named the area 'The Pearl' because of the huge, smooth, rounded granite hills near the town, the Khoikhoi people referred to it as 'Tortoise Mountains'.

One of the most influential wine makers and distributors in the country, KWV (Kooperatieve Wynbouwers Vereeniging) is based in Paarl. The town focuses on wine farming, but various other forms of agriculture are also important. There are a lot of wine cellars in the region, many with excellent restaurants. The Huguenot settlers played an important role in the development of winemaking in the region.

Paarl also has several significant monuments, the most important of these being the monuments to the Afrikaans language and culture. Afrikaans did not exist in the 17th century, and although largely based on Dutch, it includes elements of German and other languages. Paarl played a significant role in the development of the language, and the first Afrikaans newspaper was published here.

There are pleasant walks in the nearby Paarl Mountain Nature Reserve and in the gardens along the Berg River that flows past the town. Horseback riding through the mountains can also be arranged.

Paarl Tourism Bureau
Tel: (021) 872 3829.
www.paarlonline.com

The South African flag flutters over grape vines with the Paarl hills in the background

Afrikaans Language Museum
A small museum dedicated to the

history of Afrikaans. If the museum interests you, it may be worth visiting the Taal Monument, a tall, thin monument to the Afrikaans language. The monument is on the mountainside near the Paarl Mountain Nature Reserve, and has good views over the surrounding winelands.
Pastorie Ave. Tel: (021) 872 3441.
Open: Mon–Fri 9am–1pm & 2–5pm.

Paarl Museum

Contains various antiques and other displays explaining the history of the region. There are several displays that show the development of Afrikaans culture, and another section gives some of the history of mosques in the area.
303 Main St. Tel: (021) 872 2651.
www.museums.co.za
Open: Mon–Fri 9am–5pm,
Sat 9am–1pm. Closed: Sun.
Small admission charge.

Paarl Arboretum

Some lovely walks pass through this 32-hectare area of land along the Berg River. There are hundreds of species of plants and trees from the area and elsewhere in the world.
Tel: (021) 807 4500.
Open: All week.

Paarl Mountain Nature Reserve

Lovely *fynbos* vegetation dominated by massive, rounded, granite rock formations set among trees, especially wild olives. Fishing, hiking, picnics, climbing and mountain biking with great views.
Tel: (021) 872 3658 / 807 4500.

WINE NAMES

South African winemakers traditionally named their wine and wine estates after places, events or people, but times have changed, as have marketing ideas, and these days almost anything goes.

Some examples of more traditional cellar names include:

Buitenverwagting – beyond expectation.

Allesverloren – all is lost. The name was chosen after the original farmhouse burnt down. The vineyard makes some of the best port (fortified wine) in the country.

Vergenoeggd – far enough.

Wamakersvallei Winery – wagon-makers valley winery.

Some more modern names include:

Southern Right – named after the whales.

Porcupine Ridge.

Goats Do Roam.

And, perhaps the most unusual of all, *'Fat Bastard'* which is a very good chardonnay.

One of the many craft shops in the Paarl winelands

The 18th-century Cape Dutch architectural style has its own beauty and simple dignity, the Cape Dutch farmhouses being particularly impressive in their formal grouping with surrounding farm buildings.

Uniquely South African, the style is a distinct regional type, created in response to local circumstances as well as wider aspirations and more distant influences. The most characteristic feature is the distinctive gable over the main entrance. Recognisable from afar, the flamboyant gable design probably derives from the baroque architecture of the northern Netherlands. It was intended as a show of status: on houses of consequence, gables were often very richly decorated with fine plasterwork and the building's date.

The Cape Dutch farmhouse formula is simple: a single-storey, based on the H-, T- or U-plan, and built of sun-baked brick with a reed or grass thatched roof. Exterior walls were plastered with clay and whitewashed, and room sizes were determined by the lengths of beams available from local forests. In front of the main door was a raised *stoep* (terrace) of brick.

The earliest houses were simple rectangles: one room led into another with the kitchen at the far end. Later, as plans became more elaborate, the entrance door led into the *voorkamer* (front room), separated from the *agterkamer* (back room) by a decorative wooden screen. From these centrally placed rooms, doors opened to the rest of the house. Windows were usually square with wooden frames and shutters outside. Some windows were framed with wooden beams on the inside of the building. Doors in the grander buildings were very large and ornate. Some interiors were merely whitewashed, while others were decorated with wall paintings.

Interior beauty and character comes mainly from ceilings and floors which were made of massive beams and planks of yellowwood, and from panelled doors of similar material with stinkwood surrounds. In some houses, floors were of polished red Batavian tiles.

Today a large number of old Cape Dutch buildings have been carefully restored, and some are used as homes, offices and restaurants, and others as museums.

Many wine estates are built around old Cape Dutch houses and out buildings. Groot Constantia Wine Estate in Cape Town and the Boschendal Estate near Stellenbosch are excellent examples of this form of architecture. The Cape Dutch style has been copied by generations of architects, and some buildings, even though they look like the originals, are only a few years old.

Opposite: Vergelegen was founded in 1817 in Somerset West
Right: Cape Dutch furniture and antiques on display at a national monument in Tulbagh

Excursions From Cape Town

Most visitors to Cape Town spend some time travelling to destinations further afield in the region, which requires spending a few a nights away from the city. Although some of the distances may seem daunting, the roads are good, and with careful planning even relatively long trips can be very rewarding. Most towns and even some villages have tourist offices, and there are many B&Bs and other establishments with good accommodation.

Wellington church steeple

THE UPPER BREEDE RIVER VALLEY

The Upper Breede River (Afrikaans for 'wide river') is an important agricultural area, and is surrounded by mountains. The region was settled by farmers in the early 18th century, but San and Khoikhoi people had been passing through for centuries. The valley was largely cut off from Cape Town until decent roads had been built through the mountains. There are a number of vineyards and fruit farms in the valley. Horse riding, mountain biking and hiking are also popular pastimes in the region. *Allow two days. Head northeast from Cape Town on the N1 national road. After 62km (38 miles), take the Paarl exit, and follow the signs to Wellington (see information on Paarl on pp112–13).*

Grapes and other fruit grow prolifically throughout the Breede River Valley

The Breede River flows through lovely mountain and farmland scenery

Bain's Kloof Pass

The road between Paarl and Wellington traverses the spectacular Bain's Kloof Pass, built by Andrew Geddes Bain and completed in 1853. The scenery is beautiful as the road climbs the Limiteberg (the Limit mountains which were considered to be the edge of the original colony).

Wellington

Wellington is the centre of a fruit-growing and wine-making industry, and there are several cellars in the area where wine can be tasted and bought.

Wellington Museum

The museum has interesting displays reflecting the local history of the region and its various inhabitants over the years.

These include people of San, Khoikhoi, English, Scottish, Dutch and French ancestry. Oddly there is also a display of Egyptian artefacts.

Tel: (021) 873 4710.
Open: Mon–Fri 9am–5pm, Sat by appointment.
Admission charge.

Wellington Tourism Bureau

Tel: (021) 873 4604.
www.visitwellington.com

Wellington Wine Route

Contact the Tourism Bureau.

There are 32 national monuments in Church Street, Tulbagh

From Wellington, follow the R303 to where it joins the R43 to Wolseley. From there, take the R46 to Tulbagh.

Tulbagh

Church Street in Tulbagh has no fewer than 32 national monuments, all classical Cape Dutch buildings with whitewashed walls and thatched roofs, some dating back as far as 1754. Most of the cottages were severely damaged or destroyed in a rare earthquake in 1969, but were all lovingly restored to their former glory. The area also has many wine estates, restaurants and B&Bs.

The more energetic can take horseback or bicycle rides through the pretty valley, or undertake hikes of varying difficulties.

Oude Kerk Volksmuseum

The church was built in 1743, and is part of the museum complex of three buildings. The museum tells the story of Tulbagh including that of the 1969 earthquake and the reconstruction of the village.
Church St. Tel: (023) 230 1041.
Open: Mon–Fri 9am–5pm, Sat 11am–4pm & Sun 11am–4pm.
Admission charge.

The Old Drostdy Museum

The building dates back to the start of the 19th century, and was used as the *landdrost's* (magistrate's) home. The museum contains a collection of local artefacts.
Van der Stel St. Tel: (023) 230 0203.
Open: Mon–Sat 10am–12.50pm & 2–4.50pm.
Closed: Sun.
Admission charge.

Tulbagh Tourism Bureau

Tel: (023) 230 1348.

Tulbagh Wine Route
Contact the Tourism Bureau.
www.tulbaghwineroute.co.za
From Tulbagh, return on the R46 past
Wolesley, and follow the signs to Ceres.

Ceres
On the way to Ceres, the road climbs
the Mitchell's Pass. At the side of the
pass is the old tollhouse which is now
a restaurant.

Ceres is named after the Roman
goddess of fruitfulness, and is one of
South Africa's premier deciduous
fruit-growing areas.

Ceres Fruit Tours
Daily tours. Learn about fruit-growing
and taste the products. During fruit
season, Dec–Mar, tours to working
farms are arranged.

Ceres Tourism Bureau
Tel: (023) 316 1287.

Kagga Kamma Private Game Reserve
Wildlife, rock art and San cultural tours.
Tel: (021) 872 4343.
www.kaggakamma.co.za

MATJIESFONTEIN

This 19th century resort is popular with
weekenders from Cape Town. The
restored Victorian Lord Milner Hotel, and
some other buildings, in the tiny village are
national monuments. The hotel was used as
a hospital during the South African War.

The luxury Blue Train stops here on its
trip between Cape Town and Johannesburg.
The town is 260km (162 miles) from
Cape Town.

Although Matjiesfontein is fairly isolated,
some companies offer regular trips to the
settlement.

A countryside farmstall near the fruit farming area of Ceres

National monument at Tulbagh

Matroosberg Private Nature Reserve
Tel: (023) 312 2282.
Hiking, horseback riding, birding and
great mountain views.
www.matroosberg.com
*From Ceres, return over Mitchell's Pass,
and then follow the R43 to Worcester.*

Worcester

Worcester is the largest town of the
Upper Breede River Valley, and is one
of the largest grape-producing areas
of the Western Cape. The town has
excellent cellars.

Karoo National Botanical Gardens

This is an excellent place to learn about
the plants of the region. There are 10
hectares of cultivated gardens and 150
hectares of natural vegetation, including
Karoo and *fynbos* vegetation.

The gardens are situated about 3km
(1,9 miles) north of town, off the N1
national road.
Tel: (023) 347 0785.
Open: daily 8am–4pm.
Admission charge.

Kleinplasie Open Air Farm Museum

Kleinplasie (little farm) is an unusual
working museum where staff dress up
in 18th century clothes and act out life
as it was on a farm in those days.
Various activities including soap-
making, weaving, and spinning wool
take place on the property, and are
done as they would have been in the
early days.

A miniature train runs through the property at regular intervals. There is a wine cellar next door.

The musem is about one kilometre outside town on the main road to Robertson.
Tel: (023) 342 2225
Open: Mon–Sat 9am–4.30pm,
Sun 10.30am–4.30pm. Admission charge.

Worcester Tourism Bureau
Tel: (023) 348 2795.

Kleinplasie Reptile World
Crocodiles, snakes and other reptiles.
Tel: (023) 342 6840.

KWV Brandy Cellar
Tours of this brandy distillery, claimed to be the biggest of its kind.
Corner Smith St. and Church St.
Tel: (023) 342 6840.
Open: Mon–Fri 8am–4.30pm.
Admission charge.

Worcester Wine Route
Information on all wine cellars in the area.
Tel: (023) 342 8710.
www.worcesterwinelands.co.za
From Worcester, take the NI back to Cape Town – 131km (81 miles).

Homemade bread being baked in a traditional oven at the Kleinplasie Open Air Farm Museum

Copyright: South African Tourism

THE LOWER BREEDE RIVER VALLEY

The Lower Breede River Valley and surrounding areas lie alongside the Langeberg mountains. On its way to the coast, the river broadens and meanders through lovely scenery and farmlands. Some people canoe on the river, others sit alongside its banks and relax, and farmers use the water to irrigate their vineyards, fruit trees and wheat fields. Although the area is quite some way from Cape Town, this picturesque valley is worth taking the time to explore.

Allow for one or two nights away (the round trip covers at least 560km (350 miles). Take the N2 to Worcester, and then join the R60 to Robertson. Robertson is 180km (112 miles) from Cape Town.

Robertson

Robertson is the centre of yet another fruit- and wine-growing community. The vineyards and cellars are less busy than those of the winelands closer to Cape Town, but are nevertheless well geared for the tourism industry. There is a small museum in the town and good hiking in the mountains.

Robertson Tourism Bureau
Tel: (023) 626 4437.
Follow the R40 east for 19km, and take the sign-posted turn off to Montagu.

Montagu

Montagu is a favourite hiking destination, and the drive through the Kogmanskloof reveals weird rock formations and good mountain views.

The story of the Dutch East India Company (VOC) on display at the Drostdy Museum – Swellendam

The village was founded in 1851, and many of its historical buildings are national monuments. There is a popular resort with hot springs reputed to have healing properties in the town.

From Montagu, return through the pass and join the R60 to Swellendam. If you have the time, and feel like a quiet night in the countryside, return to Robertson and then take the road to McGregor, a quaint farming village of well-preserved Victorian and Cape Dutch houses in the Riviersonderend (river without end) mountains.
The round trip will add about 80km (50 miles) to your trip.

Swellendam

Although Swellendam falls into the Overberg region, it is in the valley of the Breede, and included in this tour for the sake of convenience. This town, South Africa's third oldest, is built on the slopes of the Langeberg mountains and close to the wide Breede River. This scenery helps compliment the whitewashed walls of the town's many old buildings.

The town was established in 1743 and soon after, in 1746, the building which now houses the Drostdy Museum, was constructed. The museum incorporates several other nearby buildings with displays of period furniture, clothing and art.

The Dutch Reformed Church, although only built in 1911, includes Baroque, Gothic and eastern architecture.

The nearby Marloth Nature Reserve has a network of hiking trails through the mountains. The lovely Bontebok National Park is nearby (*see p130*).

Swellendam Tourism Bureau
Tel: (028) 514 2675.
Drostdy Museum.
Tel: (028) 514 1138.
Open: daily.
From Swellendam, take the N2 to Riviersonderend. Two kilometres past Riviersonderend, take the R406 to Greyton.

Greyton

This pretty, small town has become popular with Capetonians seeking the tranquillity of the countryside. There are lovely walks around the town.

From Greyton turn right, and follow the R406 to the N2 and back to Cape Town – a further 189km (118 miles).

One of the many pretty whitewashed buildings in Greyton

Wherever you go in the Western Cape, you are likely to have to negotiate a mountain pass or two. They wind their way through spectacular fold mountains above scenic valleys, and it is sometimes worth driving through the passes simply to enjoy the views. Most have viewpoints at various strategic locations, with parking areas set off the road. Many of the roads through the passes were originally constructed in the 19th century.

Bain's Kloof Pass

Twisting and winding its way through the Hawequa Mountains, the R44 rises far above the Wit and Breede rivers glittering in the valley below. The pass was built by Andrew Geddes Bain in the 19th century, and cuts through forests and mountain *fynbos*. The highest peak in the area is the 1,633m (5,307ft) Snueekop (which in Afrikaans means 'snow peak'). This pass is near Wellington, and is about 80km (50 miles) from Cape Town.

Du Toitskloof Pass

The N1 national road goes under this pass through the 4km- (2,4 miles-) long Huguenot tunnel which was built in 1988. To enjoy the scenery of the area, take the old main road, the R101, which climbs more than 800m (2,600ft) in 10km (six miles). The Du Toitskloof Pass is between Paarl and Worcester, and is about 70km (44 miles) from Cape Town.

Franschhoek Pass

This spectacular road (the R45) winds its way from Franschhoek over the mountains to the Theewaterskloof Dam near Villiersdorp. The road climbs steeply as soon as it leaves the town, and there are various points where you can stop and look back over the beautiful valley dotted with white-gabled, thatch-roofed Cape Dutch houses surrounded by vineyards and orchards.

The road then snakes its way through the mountains, which sometimes experience winter snowfalls, with views of mountain streams far below and distant mountain peaks. There are also good views across the Theewaterskloof Dam and the surrounding farmland.

Opposite: Outeniqua Mountains, near George
Right: The Du Toitskloof Pass on the N1 national road to Cape Town

Sir Lowry's Pass

The N2 national road crosses the 1,500m- (4,875ft-) high Hottentots Holland Mountains via this pass some 55km (34 miles) from Cape Town. There are good views of Somerset West, Table Mountain and False Bay from the top of the pass.

There are two other passes that should not be missed – they are a long way from Cape Town, but worth visiting if making the trip to the Garden Route.

The Swartberg Pass

Anybody visiting the Little Karoo Ostrich Centre of Oudtshoorn should be sure to drive the Swartberg Pass which leads to the charming village of Prince Albert. The pass climbs some 800m (2,600ft) in 11km (6,8 miles) before descending steeply to Prince Albert through fantastic rock formations and cliffs.

The road offers superb views of the Little Karoo to the south,

Copyright: South African Tourism

and looks out over the Great Karoo to the north. Most of the pass road is unsurfaced. Prince Albert is about 520km (325 miles) from Cape Town, and 60km (37 miles) from Oudtshoorn.

The Prince Alfred Pass

Just outside the Garden Route town of Knysna, the R339 weaves its way through thick forest before climbing through the Klein Langkloof Mountains on the way to Uniondale. The Knysna Forest is one of the largest remaining areas of indigenous forest in South Africa, and it is worth stopping to see some of the huge yellowwood trees. They are signposted, and there are picnic sites at clearings in the forest near some of the trees (see the Garden Route on pp128–30).

Opposite top: The spectacular Swartberg Pass
Opposite bottom: All the passes offer lovely views of farmlands and indigenous vegetation
Below: The Prince Alfred Pass near Knysna

THE MOUNTAINS

Wherever you go in Cape Town and surrounding areas, there are always mountains around you. The highest point is Maclear's Beacon on Table Mountain which is 1,087m (3,532ft) above sea level. Very occasionally sleet falls on the top of the mountain.

Some other heights are:
Upper Cable Station 1,067m (3,467ft)
Devils Peak 1,001m (3,253ft)
Constantiaberg 928m (3,016ft)
  situated above Hout Bay
Lions Head 669m (2,174ft)
Paulsberg 367m (1,192ft) in the Cape
  of Good Hope Nature Reserve
Signal Hill 350m (1,137ft)

Tour: Garden Route

The Garden Route has the justifiable reputation of being one of South Africa's 'must do' drives. The road from Cape Town cuts through rolling farmlands and steep mountains before reaching the coast at Mossel Bay and heading towards the forests and mountains of George. As the road winds its way along the coast, it passes through deep river valleys, thick indigenous forest, lakes and beautiful beaches. Popular holiday towns and resorts are scattered along the coast.

A secluded cove near the Knysna Heads

Heading inland from the coast requires driving through impressive mountain passes. The region offers a wide spectrum of activities ranging from simply sunbathing and swimming, to hiking, bird watching and adventure sports. There are thousands of places to stay, and many good restaurants.

The Garden Route is very busy during the Christmas and Easter holidays.
Allow at least three days.
Start in George. It is 495km
(309 miles) from Cape Town,
along the good N2 national road.

Visitors admire the spectacular view of the Knysna Heads and the entrance to the lagoon

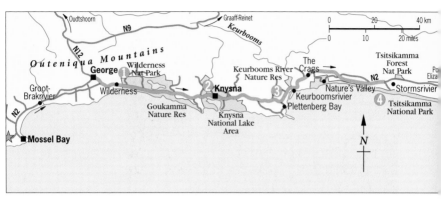

1 George and the Wilderness National Park

The town of George, which was founded in 1811, is one of the largest centres on the Garden Route, and is bordered by the forested Outeniqua mountains and lush farmlands.

The famous Outeniqua Choo-Tjoe steam train follows a spectacular route from George to Knysna, a round-trip of just under four hours, and makes a fantastic outing for all members of the family.

Just east of the town, the Wilderness National Park offers wonderful walks through peaceful countryside, past scenic coastal lakes with good views of the mountains.

Outeniqua Railway Museum and Outeniqua Choo-Tjoe

Tel: (044) 801 8288.
The museum is open Mon–Sat 8am–5pm. The train runs Mon–Sat, but call to confirm times as the schedule sometimes changes.Continue along the N2 for 62km (38 miles) to Knysna.

2 Knysna and the Prince Alfred Pass

Knysna is one of South Africa's most popular holiday towns, its huge lagoon, nearby beaches, forests and mountains attracting thousands of visitors year after year.

The high, sandstone bluffs known as 'The Heads' form a dramatic gateway between the sea and the lagoon.

There are many good beaches near Knysna including Knoetze, 10km (6,2 miles) north, which is a particular pretty beach surrounded by indigenous forest.

Nearby, the scenic Prince Albert Pass climbs through South Africa's largest patch of indigenous high forest, some 36,000 hectares (88,956 acres), containing yellowwood and stinkwood trees (*see also p127*).
Continue along the N2 to Plettenberg Bay, 44km (26 miles) away.

3 Plettenberg Bay and Robberg Peninsula

'Plett' is an upmarket, fashionable resort that overlooks a beautiful bay and

The Outeniqua Choo-Tjoe steam train runs along the coast between George and Knysna

lagoon framed by mountains in the distance. The area is well suited to relaxed beach holidays with occasional inland mountain drives. There are any number of good restaurants and shops. *Continue along the N2 to the Tsitsikamma National Park.*

4 Tsitsikamma National Park

This national park protects a spectacular 80km (50 miles) ribbon of indigenous forest deeply incised by rivers that have cut their way through the mountains to the sea. There are several huge, old yellowwood trees in the forest which can easily be viewed from well-marked trails.

The five-day Otter Trail hike takes in the area in all its splendour as the path follows the coast along high cliffs and through the forest and river crossings.

There are a large number of interesting places to visit along the borders of the park.
Otter Trail bookings can be made at **South African National Parks Central Reservations**, *and need to be made as long as a year in advance.*
Tel: (012) 248 9111.
www.parks-sa.co.za

OTHER DESTINATIONS

While driving to the Garden Route from Cape Town, it is worth considering visiting several other destinations along the way. These include the following places.

Bontebok National Park

This national park is only 8km (5 miles) from Swellendam on the N2 national road.
The Bontebok National Park was created to help save beautiful black, tan and

white bontebok antelope from extinction. The antelope had been heavily hunted ever since the first settlers arrived in Cape Town, and by the 20th century, its numbers had dwindled to the point that the conservation authorities realised they would have to act quickly if any were to survive. They have prospered in the reserve which is also home to Cape mountain zebras and a variety of smaller antelope, birds and reptiles.

The reserve also protects an important area of shrub *fynbos*, much of which has been ploughed up for wheatfields elsewhere in the region.

The park is close to Swellendam.

South African National Parks Central Reservations

Tel: (012) 428 9111.

www.parks-sa.co.za

ANGLING

The Cape offers excellent salt- and freshwater angling. Whether fishing from the beach for kob or galjoen, or from a boat for giant yellowtail or skipjack tuna, anglers will have much to choose from. Many companies charter boats and arrange fishing trips. There is also good trout fishing in Franschhoek and other mountainous regions, and the Olifants River area is a favourite destination for anglers searching for the indigenous yellowfish that is a fierce fighter when hooked.

Licences are required for all types of fishing, but are easily obtained.

Luxury holiday homes in Plettenberg Bay

Thatched fishermen cottages near the white beaches of Arniston

Cape Agulhas/Arniston

Cape Agulhas is Africa's most southerly tip, despite the commonly held belief that it is Cape Point. Nearby, the thatched-roofed and white-walled houses of Arniston have been declared a national monument, and the white, windswept beaches have a harsh beauty. Cape Agulhas is about 100km (60 miles) south of Swellendam. On the way, the Shipwreck Museum at Bredasdorp has displays of artefacts collected from the many ships wrecked along this coast.

The nearby De Hoop Nature Reserve offers protection to a wide array of vegetation, mammals and sealife. The marine reserve along the shoreline extends 5km (3 miles) out to sea. Whales are often spotted here, usually from August to October.

Witsand Tourism
Tel: (028) 537 1011.
www.witsand.com

Oudtshoorn and the Cango Caves

It's not often a bird as bizarre as the ostrich makes a town famous, but this is exactly what happened with Oudtshoorn when, in the 19th century, it became the world's largest supplier of high-fashion ostrich feathers. Although the feathers are no longer as popular in Europe as they were in the 19th and early 20th century, ostriches are still widely farmed, but these days meat and leather are the most important products derived from the huge birds.

Many farms put on ostrich shows and race them, and tourists can also ride on the long-necked creatures, the largest of the world's birds. There are good examples of Victorian buildings in the hot, sleepy town.

The Cango Caves are situated some 32km (20 miles) north of Oudtshoorn. The chambers, stalactites and stalagmites of the caves lure tourists

The spectacular interior of the Cango Caves

underground. An hour-long guided tour takes visitors through the large main caves, but the system runs much deeper under the Swartberg mountains.

Oudtshoorn Tourism Bureau
Tel: (044) 272 8226.

Cango Caves
Tel: (044) 272 7410.
Open: daily.
Admission charge and guided tours.

Prince Albert and the Swartberg Pass

The awesomely rugged Swartberg Pass lies between Oudtshoorn and the lovely small town of Prince Albert. The steep pass climbs through the Swartberg mountains, and the view across the range and the plains below is spectacular (*see also pp126–7*).

In Prince Albert, which has become a fashionable long-weekend retreat, farmers take advantage of the good water run-off from the mountains to grow grapes and olives, and the town has several good restaurants. There are lovely walks and hikes in the mountains and around the village, and the rural atmosphere makes a good breakaway destination.

A lonely farmhouse in the mountains between Oudtshoorn and Prince Albert

Prince Albert Tourism Bureau
Tel: (023) 541 1366.
*The following destinations are a long
way north of Cape Town, but again,
with careful planning, they are worth
the effort, particularly during the flower
season in early spring.*

Cedarberg Wilderness Area

The Cedarberg are a fascinating jumble
of ragged peaks, clear mountain streams
and wonderful solitude. The towns of
Citrusdal and Clanwilliam make good
bases from which to explore the
mountains and surrounding farms.
After good rains, many flowers cover the
veld, although they are not usually as

prolific as those further north in
Namaqualand.

The Cedarberg Wilderness area covers
162,000 hectares (400,302 acres), and
there are lovely guest farms and resorts
where visitors can relax and forget about
cities.

The area is about 220km (137 miles)
north of Cape Town.
Cape Nature Conservation
Tel: (027) 482 2812 for hiking permits.
www.capenature.org.za
Citrusdal Tourism Bureau
Tel: (022) 921 3210.
www.citrusdal.com
Clanwilliam Tourism Bureau
Tel: (027) 482 2361.

The weathered sandstone of the Cedarberg creates an unusual but pretty landscape

Spring flowers in the fields of Namaqualand

Olifants River Valley

The upper part of this valley begins in the Cedarberg, and then runs towards the sea past good vineyards and fruit farms. The Olifants ('elephants') Valley runs past the towns of Clanwilliam, Klawer, Vredendal and Lutzville, a distance of more than 150km (94 miles). The Olifants Valley and the Cedarberg make a good stopover on the way to Namaqualand.

Sadly the elephants, after which the river is named, were shot out in the 18th century.

Namaqualand

Every spring (roughly mid-August to mid-September), this usually hot and harsh region is transformed into a sea of colour by millions of blooming daisies and other flowers.

The towns of Springbok, Garies and Hondeklip Baai (Hondeklip Bay) are usually the best starting points from which to see the flowers, but it is worth checking with authorities first to find out where rain has fallen.

Springbok is also a good point from which to visit the remote Richtersveld National Park which is botanically unusual with many rare species. It is 521km (325 miles) from Cape Town. The mountain-desert scenery is arid, rocky and cut by jagged ravines. It is home to the semi-nomadic Nama people who have recently won back the right to graze their animals and run some tourist concessions in the park.

De Beers run tours and 4X4 trips to their rich diamond mining concessions along restricted areas of the remote, windswept western coastline which has a large population of Cape fur seals.

De Beers Diamond Coast Tours
Kleinsee.
Tel: (027) 807 2999.

Adventure Tourism

Whether you fancy jumping off bridges, diving with sharks or abseiling down cliffs, Cape Town and the Western Cape has something for all adrenaline junkies. The mountains and sea combine to offer a wide range of activities, and tourism operators have been quick to exploit these natural opportunities that provide so many ways to scare yourself silly.

Whitewater rafting on a Cape river

There are companies and organisations with good safety records that specialise in all the activities listed below. Always contact local tourism authorities or South Africa Tourism (*see Directory on pp187–8*) for recommended companies before booking an activity.

Abseiling

There are any number of mountains and cliffs on the Peninsula that are suitable for abseiling, but the most popular is, unsurprisingly, Table Mountain. The most common abseil allows tourists to drop 110m (360ft) down the face of the mountain with great views of the beaches and buildings far below. Another popular abseil is down the side of Kamikaze Canyon in the Steenbras River Gorge about 50km (31 miles) from Cape Town.

Bungee Jumping

The best spots are on the Garden Route, the most popular of which are the Gourits River Bridge and the Bloukrans River Bridge jumps. The latter is reportedly the highest commercial jump in the world, where jumpers drop a heart-stopping 215m (697ft). The Bloukrans Bridge is near Plettenberg Bay.

Climbing

There are dozens of climbs in the Western Cape mountains ranging from mere scrambles to technical ascents. Experienced climbers can contact the Mountain Club of South Africa through their own clubs.

Diving

Although the water off Cape Town is cold, diving is a popular sport, and several companies cater for all levels of diving experience. Most locals use at least a 5mm (and preferably a 7mm) wetsuit. Qualified divers should remember their logbooks. Highly qualified instructors run courses for beginners, but this takes more time than many holiday-makers have available.

Kiteboarding

Good winds along the coast and decent-sized waves make for excellent kiteboarding if you are strong enough to hold on to the kite. The kites used in this spectacular sport create a very strong drag and should only be used by experienced kiteboarders.

Kloofing (Canyoning)

There are various kloofs (canyons) near Cape Town suitable for kloofing which entails climbing along cliffs, jumping into rivers and then swimming. Lots of people enjoy doing this.

Ocean Kayaking

Several companies take guided tours along the dramatic coastline. Most trips are quite easy, and are conducted by experienced guides. There is a fair chance of spotting seals and dolphins on these trips. The Langebaan Lagoon, north of Cape Town, offers easy and safe kayaking.

Paragliding and Hang Gliding

For the experienced, this is a wonderful way to enjoy the magnificent Cape Town scenery. There are launching sites on Lions Head, Signal Hill, Kommetjie and elsewhere in the Peninsula.

River rafting

The deep river valleys cutting through the mountains of the western and southern Cape create good conditions for river rafting.

Some rivers have good whitewater rapids, particularly in the winter rainy season.

Shark Diving

Gansbaai, about 150km (93 miles) from Cape Town, is considered by many to be one of the best places in the world to dive with great white sharks. Divers are protected by steel cages.

These sharks can grow to over six metres (19ft) in length and weigh more than 1,200kg (2,600lb). From boats, other tourists watch the sharks, which prey on seals in the area.

Skydiving

This is another good way, for those with a head for heights, to enjoy the Cape's scenery. Novice jumpers can arrange tandem jumps with instructors. Various companies arrange jumps throughout the Western Cape.

A paraglider slowly descends towards Camps Bay Beach

Capetonians, like many other South Africans, love sport, and they vocally support their favourite team. At Super 12 rugby matches, the chant of 'pro-vince' is still common, although the top team is now known as 'The Stormers' and no longer Western Province, from whence the chant is derived.

The Newlands Cricket ground is well known for its scenic beauty and cheerful, cheekily humorous crowd. Elsewhere in Cape Town soccer crowds back the European-sounding Ajax and Hellenic teams.

When Bafana Bafana (The Boys), South Africa's soccer team, loses a match, the event immediately sparks radio talk-show discussions, letters to newspapers and heated debate in bars, on buses and on street corners.

Most sporting nations are passionate about their favourite team, but in South Africa losses and victories take on a special edge because sport here often has a political sub-plot.

For decades, Black players were barred from participating in top teams, and sports administrators are

still trying to ensure that equal opportunities are offered to all in terms of training, facilities and financial backing.

Sports fans are eager for success because of long-denied international competition due to sports boycotts imposed in protest against apartheid – woe betide the teams that don't fulfil these aspirations.

At the top end, sports stadiums and facilities are world class, and the nation has hosted the Rugby World Cup, Cricket World Cup, Africa Cup of Nations (soccer), the Africa Games (athletics) and several internationally important golf tournaments during the last 10 years.

Opposite: South Africa has one of the world's top cricket teams, and plays regular Test matches

Above: Soccer is by far the most popular sport in South Africa

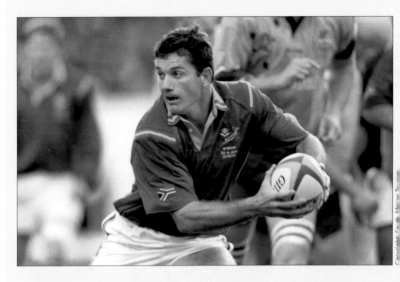

Soccer is by far South Africa's most popular sport. Across-the-nation television, and particularly in poorer and rural areas, radio, keeps millions up-to-date on important matches, both local and international.

As is the case with soccer matches anywhere, attending a big match is a raucous affair, and fans, some in fancy dress, with whistles and blow bugles to urge on their team.

Rugby fans are no less passionate, and the national team has a hundred-year-old reputation of being one of the toughest and best in the world, a reputation that is sometimes hard to live up to in the demanding world of professional sport.

Traditionally dominated by White Afrikaans-speakers, rugby is changing its profile to be more representative, and one of its defining moments was Nelson Mandela holding the World Cup with victorious captain Francois Pienaar in 1995.

Cricket is another sport in which South Africa has excelled, and it is a sport that is also changing its racial profile to become more representative.

Athletics and **boxing** are also popular, and South Africans have performed well on the international stage. Many athletes participate in the professional athletic circuits in Europe and Asia.

The country's long-distance runners are particularly successful, and a large numbers of marathons are organised every year.

South Africans have consistently been listed among the world's top **golfers**, although the sport has fairly limited appeal because of the cost of playing the game regularly.

As is befitting in a country with lots of sunshine, **watersports** are widespread. Many people water-ski on inland lakes and dams on weekends, much to the annoyance of others participating in the far more leisurely, but hugely popular, **fishing**.

Other ball sports include basketball, field hockey, bowls, netball and tennis.

South Africans also enjoy gambling, and most large cities host regular **horse race** meetings.

Opposite: Rugby is one of South Africa's most popular sports
Above: South Africa has many world-class golf courses
Left: Rugby has a fanatical following in South Africa

SOCCER WORLD CUP

South Africa will host the 2010 Soccer World Cup, one of the world's most popular sporting events.

The tournament attracts hundreds of thousands of fans, and is expected to provide a huge boost to the South African economy with a simultaneous increase in other forms of tourism. The country has many excellent soccer and rugby stadiums (which are often also used for soccer matches), and others will be renovated to cope with the expected influx of visitors.

Soccer is the most popular sport in Africa where South Africa's hosting of the Cup is regarded as particularly prestigious.

Shopping

Whether you are looking for expensive jewellery, a special gift from Africa, or merely a cheap souvenir, Cape Town has a huge variety of shops and markets to browse through. Prices according to location: shopping malls and high streets, particularly those in tourist areas, tend to be the most expensive; market stalls less so, and roadside vendors are the cheapest. But just as the prices vary, so does quality, and shoppers should be cautious before buying at the roadside.

African art and vibrant colours influence the design of many handcrafts

The Waterfront development is a very popular shopping destination, but prices, particularly those of curios, may be lower than in Long Street or Greenmarket Square. Conversely, while you are unlikely to find top-quality jewellery in Greenmarket Square, the Cavendish Shopping Centre Square will have everything from diamonds and emeralds to platinum and gold. Market and roadside vendors expect you to bargain, but shop owners in upmarket malls are less flexible and seldom oblige with lower prices.

A huge variety of curios and gifts are sold throughout the Western Cape

Many shops, such as these at Tsitsikamma, accept credit cards, and some also take travellers' cheques

WHERE TO SHOP
Antiques

Antique Cape Dutch furniture made from yellowwood or stinkwood are among the most valued antiques from the region. Prices have risen considerably in recent years, but good items can still be found. South Africa is also a good hunting ground for those who collect militaria, and many dealers have interesting collections of uniforms, medals, weapons and other items related to the armed forces.

There is also a good range of books related to Africa available.

Many antique dealers sell quality items from elsewhere in the world too. The **South African Antique Dealers' Association** *can supply a list of the better shops.*
Tel: (011) 880 2387.
www.saada.co.za

Groot Constantia Antique and Collectables Market

Held on weekends, weather permitting. All sorts of items ranging from horseshoes and silverware to books and shoes are sold.
Groot Constantia Wine Estate, Constantia. Tel: (021) 689 3908.

Long Street Antique Arcade

There are 12 antique shops in the arcade. Some have a good range of items, but others are more inclined towards selling odds and ends.
127 Long St, Cape Town.
Tel: (021) 423 3585.

Wellington Antiques

Particularly good for Cape Dutch furniture.
46 Church St, Wellington.
Tel: (021) 873 2397.

Shops stock everything from A – Z. In this case African art to zebra skins!

Ye Olde Artifact Cove & Shipwreck Shop
An off-beat collection of items, many from boats and ships. Other memorabilia too.
Mariner's Wharf, Hout Bay.
Tel: (021) 790 1100.
www.marinerswharf.com

Books and Maps
Exclusive Books and CNA stores have branches in Cape Town and throughout the country.
See the Cape Town telephone directory.

Clarke's Bookshop
Rare and second-hand books, prints and maps. Particularly good for Africana.
277 Long St, Cape Town.
Tel: (021) 423 5739.
www.clarkesbooks.co.za

Quagga Art and Books
Wide range of antiques and books.
84 Main Rd, Kalk Bay.
Tel: (021) 788 2752.

Wordsworth
Good variety of contemporary books.
Gardens Centre, Gardens.
Tel: (021) 461 8464.

Clothing
Jenni Button
High-fashion clothing for women, usually designed by South Africans (two shops).
Cavendish Square Shopping Centre, Claremont.
Tel: (021) 683 9504.
Victoria Wharf,
V & A Waterfront.
Tel: (021) 421 1346.

Homemade products on sale at a flea market at Betty's Bay

Naartjie

South African designed kids' clothing.
Victoria Wharf, V & A Waterfront.
Tel: (021) 421 5819.

Curios, Arts & Crafts and Silverware

African Image

Variety of curios and collectables.
Corner Church St and Burg St,
Cape Town.
Tel: (021) 424 2957.

Carrol Boyes

Functional art usually made from metals.
Victoria Wharf, V & A Waterfront.
Tel: (021) 418 0595.

Clementina Ceramics and Fine Art

Well-known South African ceramics.
31 Breda St, Oranjezicht.
Tel: (021) 462 5226.
www.clementina.co.za

Heartworks

South African ceramics, beadwork and other items for the home.
98 Kloof St, Cape Town.
Tel: (021) 424 8419.

Life on Long

Broad collection of crafts and art.
161 Long St, Cape Town.
Tel: (021) 461 8464.

Still Life

Unusual gifts and other items.
229c Long St, Cape Town.
Tel: (021) 426 0143.

Jewellery and Gemstones

Olga Jewellery Design Studio

Top of the range jewellery designer.
Victoria Wharf, V & A Waterfront.
Tel: (021) 419 8016.

A tourist searches for souvenirs to take home

Uwe Koetter
Top of the range jewellery.
Shop 14, Alfred Mall, V & A Waterfront.
Tel: (021) 421 1039.

Music
There are large numbers of illegally
copied CDs and DVDs for sale at
markets and even at the roadside.
Many of these are produced in the East.
While they are much cheaper than those
available at reputable stores, it is illegal
to sell them in South Africa.

The African Music Store
A broad choice of music from
around Africa.
90a Long St, Cape Town.
Tel: (021) 426 0857.

Outdoor Equipment
Cape Union Mart
Lots of gear for all forms of outdoor
activities – camping, hiking and so on.
Victoria Wharf, V & A Waterfront.
Toll free 0800 034 000.
Branches nationwide.

Surf Centre
Beach and casual clothing, wetsuits
and the like. Primarily women's wear
but has a men's section.
45 On Castle Building, Castle St,
Cape Town.
Tel: (021) 423 7853.

Shopping Malls
Canal Walk
Hundreds of shops, cinemas and
restaurants.
Tel: 0860 101 165.
www.canalwalk.co.za

Cavendish Square
High-quality shopping, cinemas and
restaurants.
Dreyer St, Claremont.
Tel: (021) 657 5600.
www.cavendish.co.za

V & A Waterfront
Hundreds of shops, cinemas and
restaurants.
Dock Rd, V & A Waterfront.
Tel: (021) 408 7600.
www.waterfront.co.za

Wild Animal Products
Various wild animal products including
trophies, skins, leather belts and shoes
are sold at markets and in shops.
Whatever one's view on buying
these products, it should be
remembered that many countries

Shopping for jewellery in Hermanus

have strict rules concerning the importation of animal products. It is also illegal to sell ivory and some other animal products including the skin of the African rock python.

Should you be offered ivory or any other animal product you suspect to be illegal, it is best to notify the police or conservation authorities. Youngsters at the side of the road commonly sell tortoises, but this trade is illegal and should be reported.

Wines

There are many excellent wine stores in Cape Town, but it is more fun to explore the vineyards and buy directly from the producers. Nearly all cellars are willing to ship wine overseas. Local wines are usually a good buy in comparison with international prices. Wine dealers will also be able to advise on customs' limitations on quantities that may be imported to various countries.

Vaughn Johnson's Wine and Cigar Shop

If you don't have time to visit the winelands, try this store for bargain prices.
Dock Rd, V & A Waterfront.
Tel: (021) 419 2121.

A shopkeeper makes the most of a quiet moment, and catches up on the news

Entertainment

Cape Town offers visitors a wide array of entertainment that mirrors the cultures and traditions of South Africa's people. Music and theatre often take on cross-cultural flavours, although Shakespeare, traditional Western theatre, classical music and opera are firm favourites in some circles. In recent years, the government has paid particular attention to encouraging the performing arts, and many young people and others from disadvantaged areas have been assisted through educational and other grants.

Jazz is hugely popular in Cape Town

Booking Tickets
Most theatre, opera, ballet and cinema tickets can be bought through Computicket which has offices nationwide. Many sports match tickets can also be booked here.

Computicket
Open: Mon–Fri 9am–5pm, Sat 9am–4pm. Cash or credit cards. They also handle on-line and telephonic booking. www.computicket.com
Nationwide Call Centre
Tel: 083 915 8000 or (011) 340 1000. Call 083 131 for information.

Listings
Check local daily newspapers for listings' sections. The national *Mail&Guardian* newspaper, published Fridays, gives excellent coverage to major cities.

The *Mail&Guardian* also has a very good entertainment section on its website *www.mg.co.za*.

Also read the *Cape Times*, *The Argus* and *The Weekend Argus*. Most regional tourism websites have links to 'what's on' in their areas.

Dress
Theatre and operagoers usually dress fairly smartly, but leave their 'best clothes' for opening nights. In clubs people wear whatever they feel like, or whatever they think their friends think they should wear!

BALLET AND DANCE
Cape Town and the Western Cape have a small but thriving ballet-loving community.

Ticket office at the Evita se Perron theatre

Fast-foods keep many people on the go throughout the day

The Artscape and Baxter theatre complexes often present highly rated professionally produced ballets featuring some of the country's best dancers. Internationally acclaimed dancers often visit too. In the suburbs and smaller towns of the region, ballet classes are common.

Ballroom dancing is extremely popular, particularly in townships, and children and adults compete in regular competitions. Many people spend considerable amounts of money on classes and their dancing clothes to ensure their competitiveness.

Traditional African dancing is also part of the dance culture of Cape Town, and many theatre and musical productions incorporate Xhosa, Zulu, Tswana or other local dancing styles.

BARS AND PUBS

As is to be expected, there are a huge number of bars and pubs. In Cape Town, nearly all offer food and drink, but in a sports-mad country it's the establishments that screen live sports matches that get really packed.

In these pubs and bars most of the important international rugby, cricket and soccer matches are screened live, and the atmosphere in the better venues is

Relaxing at the end of a hard day's touring

second only to being at the game. The partisan fans welcome anyone who enjoys sport.

Golf, Formula One racing and English soccer are also regularly screened, as are special events including the Olympics and the Tour de France.

The more seriously sports-oriented pubs show the matches on big screens.

Cape Town
The Fireman's Arms
Fun 1906 vintage bar with great atmosphere.
25 Mechau St, City Bowl.
Tel: (021) 419 1513.

The Sports Café
Screens a wide variety of international sport with the more important contests being shown live.
Upper Level, Victoria Wharf.
Tel: (021) 419 5558.

Cafés line the Waterfront

CINEMA
Cape Town has become an important player in the South African film industry, and many international and local companies take advantage of the region's scenic beauty. The city is also used as a location for feature films and advertising shoots. The South African film industry has grown considerably in recent years, and local films sometimes attract more audiences than multi-million dollar Hollywood productions.

Perhaps the most successful contemporary South African director

Copyright: South African Tourism

The band gears up for a night of entertainment at a club in Cape Town

is Leon Schuster whose *skop, skiet en donner* ('kick, shoot and bash') style of slapstick humour is hugely popular.

Most large centres hold regular film festivals, details of which are usually listed in local newspapers and on tourism authority websites.

Ster-Kinekor and Nu Metro, the two largest distributors of films in South Africa, have screens all over the country. Nearly all these cinemas are located in shopping malls, and most local newspapers publish movie listings.

Ster-Kinekor
Tel: 082 16789
www.sterkinekor.com
Nu Metro
Tel: 086 1100 220
www.numetro.co.za

Some cinemas, which are not part of the major commercial networks, often show foreign and 'art' films not distributed on circuit. These include the following cinemas.

Cape Town
IMAX
Visually stunning large format screen, which usually shows spectacular wildlife events.
V & A Waterfront. Tel: (021) 419 7365.

The Iziko-SA National Gallery
Sometimes shows documentaries and films by local independent filmmakers. Check their listings' sheets.
Government Ave. Tel: (021) 456 1628.

The Labia
A favourite Cape Town venue. Fashionably laid back with a bar downstairs.
Orange St, Gardens. Tel: (021) 424 5927.

The Labia theatre is one of the oldest and most popular in Cape Town

MUSIC

Jazz is particularly popular in Cape Town, but most people will find some musical form that suits their taste in the bars, clubs and theatres of the city. West and central African influences are common in many live club performances, but reggae, rock 'n roll, and even country & western music pops up all over the city too.

The younger generation favour *kwaito* (the South African form of rap), trance, house and general pop. Check the local paper to see what is on offer. Occasionally rock concerts featuring international and local stars are hosted at sports stadiums or indoor arenas.

Opera and classical music are often performed in the larger cities, sometimes in the grand old buildings built as city halls.

Cape Town
Cape Town City Hall

Classical music and opera in grand surroundings.
Darling St. Tel. (021) 410 9809.
www.capephilharmonic.org.za

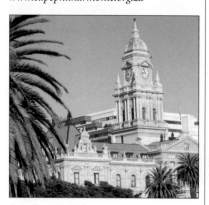

Cape Town City Hall

Green Dolphin

Live jazz and dining.
V & A Waterfront.
Tel: (021) 421 7471.
www.greendolphin.co.za
Open: all week.

Mannenberg's Jazz Café

Live jazz and dining.
Clock Tower Centre, V & A Waterfront.
Tel. (021) 421 5639.
Open: all week, music usually from 8.30pm.

Open-air venues
Kirstenbosch Summer Sunset

Concerts, jazz, classical music, choirs. In winter the visitor centre hosts indoor concerts weekly.
Kirstenbosch National Botanical Gardens, Rhodes Dr, Newlands.
Tel: (021) 799 8783.
www.nbi.ac.za

Oude Libertas Amphitheatre

Classical music and dance.
Adam Tas Rd, Stellenbosch.
Tel: (021) 809 1111.
www.oudelibertas.co.za

THEATRE

As with music, theatre in South Africa reflects the diversity of the population. A Chekov play may be running at one theatre, while a John Kani production is on at the next, and some other theatre work that falls into no particular camp will also attract audiences.

Much of South Africa's modern theatre has drawn on the experiences of the political struggle, although many playwrights are now exploring new themes.

Cape Town
Artscape Theatre Centre
This large complex hosts some of
Cape Town's biggest theatre, ballet,
opera, and classical music productions.
D F Malan St, Foreshore.
Tel: (021) 410 9801.
www.artscape.co.za

Independent Armchair Theatre
This theatre tends to feature alternative
and younger performers, often comedians
and actors exploring new trends.
135 Main Rd, Observatory.
Tel: (021) 447 1514.

The Baxter Theatre Centre
'The Baxter' is one of Cape Town's best-
known centres of theatre and ballet.
Main Rd, Rondebosch.
Tel: (021) 685 7880.

Theatre on the Bay
A relaxed and informal theatre where
nobody minds if you sip your wine
while watching the show.
1 Link St, Camps Bay.
Tel: (021) 438 3301.

Darling
Evita se Perron
Pieter Dirk Uys, South Africa's foremost
satirist, and the bane of many a politician,
runs the theatre and performs too. In
recent years, he has contributed an
enormous amount of effort towards
AIDS education.
Darling Station, Arcadia Rd, Darling –
about an hour's drive north of Cape Town.
Tel. (022) 492 2851.
www.evita.co.za

CASINOS

Although a relatively new
phenomenon in South Africa (they
were outlawed prior to 1994) casinos are
hugely popular, and the spinning wheels
and bright light attract thousands of
hopeful customers daily. The casinos, and
accompanying hotels, tend to be situated
near the larger cities, but operate in all
nine provinces. Some of the larger casinos
are part of big shopping complexes, or
have other attractions including
amusement parks nearby.

South Africa also has a national lottery,
The Lotto, for which winners are selected
every Wednesday and Saturday.

Baxter Theatre Complex

Children

Cape Town is a 'children-friendly' city for visitors, and there is a wide range of activities and entertainment available all year round. During the holiday seasons, the tourism authorities, shopping centre managers and others arrange special entertainment for children of all ages. In general, South Africa's good climate and open spaces make it a pleasant place for children to visit.

A youngster testing the water

In the cities, many teenagers hang out in shopping malls where they can go to the movies, chat with their friends or get something to eat in safety.

In many cases the 'kids culture' is very American, and Hollywood movies, television, pop stars and even fast-food often have an American orientation.

Travelling with Small Children

In Cape Town, and elsewhere in South Africa, all the essentials from disposable nappies to DVDs are widely available.

Bear in mind that if you are travelling, distances between locations can be very long, so carry books and

Kids having fun in the sun

The imaginative use of old farm implements provides entertainment for children near Stellenbosch

games. Many South African parents resort to allowing their children to play endless cell phone games to ease the boredom.

There are excellent service stations on most major routes, and these have clean toilets, fast-food outlets and general stores. Some even have small gardens where children can use up surplus energy. Many South African fast-food and family restaurants have children's menus.

Swimming
Currents along the South African coast can be powerful and unpredictable. Never allow children to swim unattended. Many more popular beaches have lifeguards, but the coastline is long, and it is not possible to patrol it all. Some beaches have tidal pools that make for safe swimming. Make sure that children refresh their sunblock regularly.

National Parks
Most camp sites in national parks and nature reserves are fenced, and are quite safe for children, but it is best to adopt a 'look, but don't touch' policy with regard to wildlife. Even small animals such as mongooses or vervet monkeys, that sometimes hang around campsites and seem quite tame, are strong and fast and can inflict painful bites if they feel threatened.

Insects – Bites and Stings
See under Health on p181.

Hotels
Some hotels can arrange a babysitting service. Both local and satellite TV services have a selection of children's programmes.

There is a wide range of entertainment parks, playgrounds and children-orientated activities available in most cities and towns.

Sport and Leisure

Sport is a way of life for many Capetonians and South Africans, and the subject often dominates newspapers, television schedules and conversations. On weekends, tens of thousands of people participate in a wide range of sports, and then go on to watch big matches on television. Ball sports are by far the most popular, but Cape Town's coastline and mountains encourage surfing, diving, hiking and other energetic activities. Sports facilities are generally very good, although some areas have been neglected.

Cape Town's wonderful scenery encourages all kinds of outdoor activities

The Argus Cycle Race

The Argus cycle race is one of the largest in the world, and every year in April some 34,000 cyclists follow the spectacularly scenic 106km (66 miles) course that treats participants to stunning views of the mountains, sea and beaches.

The Argus Cycle Race attracts people from all over South Africa and an increasing number of foreigners

Copyright: South African Tourism

Milnerton Golf Course offers impressive views of Table Mountain

Cyclists from across the country, and some from as far afield as Europe, compete in the race. The event is more than simply a race, and has turned into a social event too – a sort of giant reunion party of old friends and competitors.

Most accommodation in the city is booked out long before the race. After the race is finished, restaurants are usually packed with people, many still in their racing gear, relaxing and recounting their two-wheeled exploits.

The Two Oceans Marathon

This is another event where athletes enjoy great views, if they are fit enough, while they push their bodies to the limit. Along the way, runners from all over southern Africa have views of both the Atlantic and Indian oceans, hence the name of the race.

This is one of the premier events on the road-running calendar, and an important 'sister' race to the famous 91km (56 miles) Comrades Marathon run in KwaZulu-Natal between Durban and Pietermaritzburg.

Sports Bodies and Venues

South Africa has world-class sporting facilities, and the cricket, rugby, soccer and athletics stadiums compare with the best, and Cape Town is no exception. All the cities and many smaller towns also have excellent golf courses.

A comprehensive list of all the sporting bodies in South Africa can be found on the website of the South African Sports Commission. The website includes contact numbers, scheduled meetings or matches, officials and venues. It is particularly good for helping plan which events to attend.

South African Sports Commission
Tel: (012) 677 9746.
www.sasc.org.za

The Government's Department of Sports and Recreation
Tel: (012) 465 5506.
www.srsa.gov.za

Contact Details for Major Sports
Athletics South Africa
Tel: (011) 880 5800.
www.athleticssa.co.za

Equestrian Association of South Africa
Tel: (012) 803 9351.
www.thsinfo.co.za

Motor Sport South Africa
Tel: (011) 466 2440.
www.motorsport.co.za

South African Cycling Federation
Tel: (012) 800 2759.
www.sacf.co.za

South African Football Association
Tel: (011) 494 3522.
www.safagoal.net

South African Golf Association
Tel: (011) 785 4203.
www.saga.co.za

South African Rugby Football Union
Tel: (021) 659 6900.
www.sarugby.net

United Cricket Board of South Africa
Tel: (011) 880 2810.
www.ucbsa.co.za

GOLF

An increasing number of tourists are taking advantage of good weather and cheap rates to play on South Africa's championship-standard golf courses.

Many exclusive housing estates have been constructed recently around courses designed by golfing legends Gary Player and Jack Nicklaus among others.

The Fancourt Country Estate near George on the Garden Route, and the Erinvale Course in Somerset West are among the best in the country. Most courses accept visitors, and green and caddy fees are far below those common in Europe and the United States. Others, including the Milnerton Course in Cape Town, are particularly challenging when the wind is blowing. Regional tourism authorities and hotels will have details of how to book a round.

Copyright: South African Tourism

An angler tries his luck while the sun sets over the mountains

Capetonians make the most of their many beaches and good weather

Food and Drink

The cuisine of the Cape is influenced by Africa, Europe and the East, and is in many cases a blend of flavours adapted from diverse cooking styles. Many South Africans are meat-eaters, and beef, lamb, chicken and pork form the basis of numerous dishes. South African red meat is excellent, and is cheap by European standards. Fresh seafood is widely available and hugely popular. Wine is the drink of choice for many in the Cape, although beer is also a firm favourite.

Menu offering local delights

SOUTH AFRICAN SPECIALITIES
Biltong

Biltong (savoury dried meat) is more than a snack food for many South Africans; it's almost a cult item. Connoisseurs will debate the fat content,

composition of the spices and moisture content. It's like wine-tasting for beer-drinking sports fans.

Biltong is sold all over South Africa. It is eaten while having a drink in a bar, watching a rugby match on

Lunch time at the Waterfront, with hungry seagulls waiting their turn

TV or pretty much anytime someone feels like a salty snack.

It is usually made from beef or game animals including kudu and eland. Ostrich meat is also used.

Strips of raw meat are usually dipped in vinegar, coated in ground coriander seed, black pepper and salt, and then hung in a cool, dry place to cure. Under the right circumstances, it is ready after a few days, and is usually cut into thin slices.

The early Dutch settlers originally used the recipe as a means of preserving meat.

Bobotie

Bobotie is ground lamb flavoured with turmeric, cinnamon and other spices covered with a form of custard and baked in the oven. It is usually served with yellow rice, raisins and stewed fruit.

Boerewors

Boerewors (in Afrikaans 'farmers' sausage') is a favourite among many South Africans. It consists of homemade sausage filled with a variety of meats and spices.

Bunny Chow

Many Capetonians happily follow their compatriots in Durban in viewing a bunny chow as a good, cheap, spicy meal. And it has nothing to do with rabbits. A half-loaf of square-shaped bread is hollowed out and filled with meat or vegetable curry, and the inside of the loaf is then used to scoop the curry out.

Koeksisters

Koeksisters are favourites among Afrikaans-speaking people, and are fried dough dipped in very sweet syrup.

THE BRAAI

In simple terms a braai is a barbecue where meat, poultry, fish or vegetables, or all of them, are grilled over an open fire. The braai is a whole cultural experience that is popular in all sectors of the population. As with the potjie, everyone has their own idea as to the perfect recipe and method, but in the end the braai serves the same purpose for all – it's a great way to socialise, relax and enjoy good weather. Beer, wine and other drinks usually accompany the event.

You will find South Africans having a *braai* in the lush gardens of Camps Bay in Cape Town, and in the dusty streets of Uniondale in the Little Karoo. Almost everyone '*braais*'.

Copyright: South African Tourism

An impromptu braai in the park

Mealies

Mealies (maize on the cob) roasted over an open brazier are a popular snack food for many South Africans. They can often be bought on street corners, particularly in Gugulethu, Nyanga and other townships. The cobs are usually quite crisp and chewy.

Pap and Vleis

Pap en vleis (firm porridge and meat) is the favourite fast-food of many South Africans. The meat is usually barbecued or grilled, and the pap is a firm porridge made from de-husked maze and served with gravy. Pap is as popular among Zulu- and Xhosa-speaking people as it is in Afrikaans-speaking communities. In various forms, it is found throughout southern and east Africa.

In Zulu it is called *phutu*, among Zimbabweans it is *sadza* and in parts of Zambia it is called *ntshima* – in short most people eat it. Some people prefer it moist, some dry, others like it with sour milk and others gravy.

Potjiekos

This is meat and vegetables cooked in a heavy cast-iron, three-legged pot. The pot (*potjie* – pronounced poy-key) is placed over open coals, and the stew is left to simmer for hours. Everyone has their own recipe and method, and will stoutly defend their way of cooking a *potjie* as being the only way to do so.

Prawns Peri-peri

Brought to South Africa byPortuguese visitors from Mozambique, theprawns are coated in olive oil, lemon juice, garlic and peri-peri (hot ground chillies) and then grilled.

Sosaties

Sosaties (kebabs) are lamb, beef or even vegetables skewered, and usually *braaied* on an open fire.

A country restaurant in the hamlet of Prince Albert

Wine-lovers at Vergelegen estate

Smoorsnoek

Smoorsnoek (smoked snoek) is a typical Cape Malay dish made with a large predatory fish, similar to a barracuda, called snoek, that has been smoked over oak. Chilli, onions, potatoes and sometimes tomato are added, and it is usually served with some form of chutney or jam.

Waterblommetjie Breedie

This waterlily stew is made from lamb and the buds of the indigenous water lily (*waterblommetjie*) – a speciality of the Western Cape.

Seafood delicacies

WHERE TO EAT AND DRINK
Price guide
* = main course
   up to R65
** = up to R85
*** = over R85

Cape Town
Blues**
Trendy seafood restaurant right over the road from Camps Bay Beach.
Victoria Rd, Camps Bay.
Tel: (021) 438 2040.

Buitenverwagting***
Old favourite situated on a lovely wine farm.
   Great place to spend an afternoon or to go for dinner.
Klein Constantia Rd, Constantia.
Tel: (021) 794 3522.

Bukhara**
The very popular traditional Indian restaurant.
33 Church St, Cape Town.
Tel: (021) 424 0000.
www.bukhara.com

Cape Colony***
A top-class formal restaurant with a formal menu and also excellent service.
Mount Nelson Hotel, Gardens.
Tel: (021) 483 1198.

Downs*
A good place for a drink while watching the sun set over Hout Bay.
1 Beach Rd, Hout Bay.
Tel: (021) 790 1876.

Durbanville Hills Winery**
Great wine and food, and an even better view of Table Mountain and Table Bay.
Tel: (021) 558 1300.
www.durbanvillehills.co.za

Ginja**
Fusion-Asian food.
121 Castle St, Cape Town.
Tel: (021) 426 2368.

Marimba**–***
African and international cuisine.
Cape Town International Convention Centre.
Tel: (021) 418 3366.
www.marimbasa.com

Miller's Thumb**
Excellent seafood.
10b Kloof Nek Rd, Tamboerskloof.
Tel: (021) 424 3238.

Savoy Cabbage**
Innovative restaurant.
101 Hout St, Cape Town.
Tel: (021) 424 2626.

Kalk Bay
Cape to Cuba**
Friendly and fun with a view of the harbour. Good seafood and old Havana décor.
Main Rd, Kalk Bay.
Tel: (021) 788 1566.

The Brass Bell*–**
Casual and laid back with great sea views and something of a tradition among Capetonians.
During bad weather, the sea spray flies against the windows of the restaurant.
Main Rd, Kalk Bay.
Tel: (021) 788 5456.

Franschhoek
Le Quartier Francais**
Lovely al fresco dining, cool in summer, but warm inside in winter.
Skilfully run with a top-class reputation.
Huguenot Rd,
Franschhoek.
Tel: (021) 876 3105.

Watching the sun set over Hout Bay is a great place for drinks

Knysna
The Oystercatcher*
Oysters fresh from the sea, and a great view of the lagoon.
Small Craft Harbour, Knysna.
Tel: (044) 382 6943.

Somerset West/Stellenbosch
96 Winery Road**
South African and international food, and excellent wine list. Winelands setting.
96 Winery Rd. On R44 between Somerset West and Stellenbosch.
Tel: (021) 842 2020.

Boschendal**-***
One of South Africa's most famous wine estates. The main restaurant offers excellent South African cuisine. Between October – May, the real treat is the picnic basket from Le Pique Nique enjoyed in the gardens with magnificent views.
Close to the junction of the R310 and R45 between Franschhoek and Paarl.
Tel: (021) 870 4200.
www.boschendal.com

Haute Cabriere Cellar Restaurant**-***
Top-class international cuisine.
Cabriere Estate. Off Daniel Hugo Road which joins R45 running through the town. Tel: (021) 876 3688.

Paarl
Bosman's**
Designer food. Excellent reputation with many local specialities. Extensive wine list.
The Grand Roche, Plantasie St, Paarl.
Tel: (021) 863 2727.
www.granderoche.com

Stellenbosch
Spier Estate*-***
Cape Malay buffet and other meals on a wine estate with lovely gardens. Café too.
Baden Powell Drive, near Stellenbosch.
Tel: (021) 809 1100.

Tulbagh
Paddagang Wine House*
Traditional Cape menu includes smoked snoek paté and sometimes *waterblommetjie breedie.*
23 Church St, Tulbagh.
Tel: (023) 230 0242.

BUYING FOOD
Carlucci's
Deli with all sorts of temptations from fresh pasta and chocolate to olive oils and wine.
Corner Upper Orange St and Montrose Ave. Tel: (021) 465 0795.

Kalk Bay Harbour
Fresh fish from the trawlers is sold on the quayside. Bargaining is brisk, and you need to shout to be heard.

Melissa's – The Food Shop
Italian and other foods.
94 Kloof St, Gardens. Tel: (021) 424 5540.
www.melissas.co.za

Décor on a restaurant wall

Hotels and Accommodation

Cape Town, as with the rest of South Africa, has a wide array of hotels, bed and breakfasts, self-catering apartments and other forms of accommodation. They range from the ultra-luxurious hotels and game lodges to self-catering apartments where you do your own cooking. The South African tourism industry has grown by leaps and bounds over the past few years, and one can usually find good accommodation even in the smaller towns.

Greyton's Toad Hall B&B

South African Tourism and the regional tourism authorities (*see Directory on pp187–8*), all have excellent websites listing accommodation. All the tourism offices are happy to help tourists find accommodation no matter what the price range.

Hotels

Hotels in Cape Town, and South Africa generally, are rated on a star basis with five stars denoting 'outstanding' or 'luxury', and at the bottom end of the scale one star indicating a no-frills establishment.

Modern hotels compete for space in the centre of Cape Town

The grand old Mount Nelson Hotel

Some hotels and B&Bs choose not to be rated, but still offer excellent value for money and service. The objective of the national grading scheme is to assist in the improvement in the overall quality of accommodation and services in South Africa. The aim is not to police or impose strict and inflexible guidelines on graded establishments.

Luxury or outstanding hotels are world class, and offer everything a guest would expect of a 'top of the range' establishment. Many are in the larger cities, but there have been a profusion of smaller 'boutique hotels' built recently in the prettier parts of the country.

The majority of the private game lodges fall into this category. They offer personalised service and top-class cooking, as well as showing off the wild residents of the area.

Top of the range hotels in Cape Town include The Table Bay, The Mount Nelson and The Bay.

Two- and three-star hotels tend to be comfortable and good value for money. These may also include some of the less exclusive game lodges. Some of the chain and business hotels also fall into this category.

B&Bs

There are large numbers of B&Bs in all the major tourist areas. Some are in people's homes where the host treats tourists as members of the family, and others are entirely self-contained cottages or houses. Most hosts will arrange dinner if requested. Breakfasts are usually fruit, cereal and toast or bacon and eggs.

There are also B&Bs in some townships, and staying there provides an insight into a very different world to that of an experience in a soulless hotel. All the tourism authorities have lists of good B&Bs.

Guesthouses tend to be converted houses or stand-alone buildings where the owner does not stay in the dwelling.

Private Game Reserves

Most private game reserves charge more than national parks, and have more luxurious accommodation. Guests usually travel within the reserves in open vehicles accompanied by professional guides.

All meals are usually provided. At private game reserves, everything from making tea to cooking supper and spotting game is usually done for guests by the staff.

National Parks and Game Reserves

Clean and comfortable chalets are the standard accommodation in most national parks and game reserves. Usually guests cater for themselves, and the chalets are equipped with a fridge, stove or hotplate, cutlery, crockery and kitchen utensils.

They almost inevitably all have *braai* (barbeque) facilities for outdoor cooking too. Most camps supply utensils and crockery, but always confirm this when booking.

The majority of these chalets have their own bathroom, but in some instances there are shared ablution blocks. They are usually spotlessly clean.

Backpackers

There are backpacker lodges in most of the bigger cities, and in some smaller towns too, particularly along the Garden

The Karoo is a wonderful destination for those wishing to spend time on farms or in game reserves, or enjoying other aspects of the great outdoors

The luxury Bay Hotel beneath the Twelve Apostles, Camps Bay

Route and elsewhere along the coast. It is not advisable to sleep on beaches or in parks.

Health Spas

There are a number of exclusive health spas set in beautiful countryside. Most have swimming pools, some have tennis courts, and there is often good mountain biking or hiking in the area. The spas cater for a wide range of taste and expenditure.

Rented Accommodation

Self-catering, serviced apartments are available for short-term rents. Some people also rent out their entire homes over holiday periods, which is an option that can be considered if tourists are travelling in a small party. Prices have increased in recent years. Tourism authorities will assist in finding rented accommodation.

Caravanning and Camper Vans

There are many caravan parks throughout the Cape. There are also beautiful sites in nature reserves and resorts. All are equipped with ablution blocks, open-air cooking facilities and electrical outlets. Several companies have camper vans to rent.

Camping

Most game reserves have campsites suitable for pitching tents. Nearly all have ablution blocks and outdoor cooking facilities.

Farm Stays

There are many B&Bs on working farms throughout the country, and spending a day or two at one is a good way to learn a bit about country life in South Africa.

To Find Accommodation

Please see websites listed under each regional tourism authority.
South Africa Tourism
Tel: (011) 895 3000.
www.southafrica.net

Place names

Many villages, rivers and mountains bear the names of animals that were shot out in the 18th and 19th centuries. They are usually in Afrikaans, and have been adapted from the original Dutch. Some of the more common names are listed below.

Animal Names

Today these animals, with the exception of the leopard, are only likely to be found in game reserves.

Buffel
Buffalo.

Leeu
Lion.

Olifant
Elephant (also sometimes spelt 'oliphant').

Qwagga
A creature similar to a zebra. The qwagga was shot to extinction in the 18th and 19th centuries.

Renoster
Rhinoceros.

Seekoi
Hippopotamus (directly translated this means 'sea cow').

Tier
Leopard (directly translated, this means tiger, but was a misnomer).

Wolve
Hyaena (directly translated, this means wolves, also a misnomer).

Area/Place Names

These are most often linked to the Afrikaans words for river, spring, mountain or plains.

Berg
Mountain.

Rivier
River.

Spruit
Spring.

Vlakte
Plains.

Opposite: Leopard
Above: Elephant
Below: The Sneeuberg, the snow mountains, in the Western Cape

Place names

Copyright: South African Tourism

Other Afrikaans names

The following are also commonly used:

Blou

Blue.

Bok

Buck, as in springbuck. People often use the English and Afrikaans terms interchangeably, i.e. springbuck or springbok, gemsbuck or gemsbok.

Copyright: South African Tourism

BIG FIVE GAME RESERVES

The Big 5 game reserves that are nearest to Cape Town are the Addo Elephant National Park and the Shamwari Private Game Reserve. Although they are some 700km 435 miles) away, near Port Elizabeth, they are much closer than the reserves of Mpumalanga, North West and KwaZulu-Natal.

So if you are not able to travel large distances, these are your best bets to see elephants, lions, buffalo, rhino and leopard. Both reserves can easily be reached in a day's drive from Cape Town. If your holiday is the only chance of seeing these animals in the bush, you should make the effort.

Bosch
Bush or wild area, as in Stellenbosch.

Dorp
Village, as in Villiersdorp – 'Villiers' village.

Klein
Small, as in Klein Constantia.

Kloof
A gorge or cutting through a mountain, as in Bain's Kloof.

Mond
River mouth, as in Kleinmond.

Rooi
Red.

Sneeu
Snow.

Strand
Beach, as in Bloubergstrand.

Swart
Black.

Opposite top: Gemsbok
Opposite bottom: Black rhino
Below left: Langeberg (long mountains)
Below: Bloubergstrand (blue mountain beach)
Below right: Kleinmond (small river mouth)

Practical Guide

ARRIVING

Documents

Visitors must hold a valid passport, endorsed with a visa if required. For information on passport and visa requirements, contact your local passport office or the diplomatic or consular representative of the South African Government. Proof is required that you can support yourself in South Africa. If you do not have a return ticket, you must show that you have the means to buy one.

By Air

International airports at Johannesburg, Cape Town and Durban have regular scheduled flights from all over the world. South African Airways (SAA) is partly owned by the state.

Airport tax is included in the price of the air ticket. These taxes are levied for both international and domestic flights.

There are regular flights from Cape Town to Johannesburg International Airport, South Africa's busiest international hub. Johannesburg International is 25km (15,5 miles) east of Johannesburg. Serving both Johannesburg and Pretoria, the airport has extensive duty-free facilities. Scheduled bus services are available between airport and city centres, taxis are readily to hand, and car rental companies are represented.

General enquiries: Tel: (011) 921 6262.

A scheduled bus service connects airport and city centre at regular intervals. This is about 20km (12,5 miles). Taxis are available and all the major car-hire companies are represented.

Flight details. Tel: (021) 934 0407.

SAA proudly flying over Table Mountain

Air France
Tel: (011) 770 1601.
www.airfrance.com.za

British Airways
Tel: (011) 441 8600 or
toll free 086 001 1747.
www.british-airways.co.za

Kulula
Domestic routes only.
Tel: toll free 086 158 58 52.
www.kulula.com

Lufthansa
Tel: (011) 484 4711 or
toll free 086 184 2538.
www.lufhthansa.com

Nationwide Airlines
Domestic routes only.
Tel: toll free 0861 737 737.
www.flynationwide.co.za

Qantas
Tel: (011) 441 8550.
www.qantas.com

South African Airways (SAA)
Tel: (011) 978 1111.
www.flysaa.com

Virgin Atlantic
Tel: (011) 340 3500.
www.virgin-atlantic.com
For other airlines, see the telephone
directory.

By Land
South Africa has land borders with
Namibia, Botswana, Zimbabwe,
Mozambique, Swaziland and Lesotho.

Cape Town is well served by regular flights

All are open at the time of writing. Visas
may be required by some nationalities.
Most border posts are not open 24 hours
a day.

The Thomas Cook Overseas
Timetable, published bi-monthly, gives
details of many rail, bus and shipping
services worldwide, and is a help when
planning a rail journey to, from and
around South Africa.
Available in the UK from some stations,
any branch of Thomas Cook, or by
phoning 01733-41677.
In the USA they are available from SF
Travel Publications, 3959 Electric Rd,
Suite 155, Roanoke, VA 24018.
Tel: 1(800) 322 3834
sales@travelbookstore.com
www.travelbookstore.com

By Sea
A number of shipping companies
provide cargo/passenger services
linking South Africa and Europe.
Various cruise-liners visit South
African ports from time to time.

Queen Elizabeth II docked in Cape Town harbour

The Safmarine shipping company have space for 12 passengers in six double cabins on each of the 'Big White' container ships that travel between Cape Town and Tilbury, UK.

The trip takes 14–16 days. If you start or continue to Durban, add another five days.
Tel: (021) 525 2470.
www.safmarine.co.za

The **RMS St Helena** travels between Cape Town, the Island of St Helena and Cardiff several times a year.
Andrew Wier Shipping.
Tel: (021) 425 1165 or UK 207 816 4800.
www.rms-st-helena.com

Permitted Imports
Currency
Only R5,000 in South African Reserve Bank notes can be imported, while unlimited foreign currency and traveller's cheques are allowed, provided they are declared on arrival. Foreign passport holders may not take out more foreign currency than they declared on arrival.

Drugs
Narcotics and habit-forming drugs are prohibited.

Duty Free Allowance
The following items are allowed duty free: 400 cigarettes, 250 grams of tobacco and 50 cigars; one litre of spirits and two litres of wine; 50ml of perfume and 250ml of eau de toilette. Also gifts, souvenirs and all other goods to the value of R500. No person under 18 is entitled to the alcohol or tobacco allowance. Duty is levied at 20 per cent thereafter.

CAMPING AND CARAVANNING
Both camping and caravanning are exceptionally good value (*see Hotels and Accommodation on pp166–9*). The local tourism bureau will supply information about sites.

CHILDREN
See pp154–5.

CLIMATE
See Geography and Climate on pp6–9.

CONVERSION TABLES
See p188.

CRIME
See p35.

DRIVING
Car Rental
Although theft and damage insurance should be bought when renting the car, most companies have a minimum 'excess charge' which is the amount you will have to pay if the car is damaged or stolen. The excess also applies to the radio/tape.

You can agree to pay a larger amount for insurance which reduces the excess. Ask about this when booking the car.

Look for rentals that offer free daily mileage if travelling long distances. Ask if the company has any special deals on offer.

You need a valid drivers' licence, and sometimes a minimum age is specified.

Avis
Toll free in South Africa. Tel: 0861 02 1111.
International calls. Tel: + 27 11 394 5433.
www.avis.com

Budget
Toll free in South Africa. Tel: 0861 01 6622.
International calls. Tel: +27 11 394 2905.
www.budget.co.za

Europcar
Toll free in South Africa.
Tel: 0800 01 1344.
International calls.
Tel: +27 11 394 1406.
www.europcar.co.za

Imperial
Toll free in South Africa.
Tel: +0861 13 1000.
International calls.
Tel: +27 11 394 4020.
www.imperialcarrental.co.za

Maui
Camper van rental.
All calls.
Tel: (011) 396 1445.
www.maui.co.za

Sani Van Rental
Toll free in South Africa.
Tel: 0861 00 2111.
International calls.
Tel: +27 11 362 2111.
www.sani.co.za

Tempest/Sixt
Toll free in South Africa.
Tel: 0860 03 1666.
International calls.
Tel: +27 11 396 1080.
www.tempestcarhire.co.za

Dollar Thrifty
Toll free in South Africa.
Tel: 0861 00 211.
International calls.
Tel: +27 11 362 2111.
www.thrifty.co.za

On the Road

The road network is excellent, and you drive on the left. The speed limit in built-up areas is 60kph (37mph), on secondary roads l00kph (62mph), and on freeways 120kph (75mph) unless otherwise indicated.

Traffic laws are strictly enforced: seat belts are compulsory; carry your driving licence; do not drive under the influence of alcohol. Before your departure, check with the Automobile Association (AA) in your country if an International Driving Permit is needed to drive in South Africa.

Filling stations are plentiful on major routes, infrequent on others. On major routes most are open 24 hours-a-day, and have excellent facilities including fast-food restaurants and toilets. Most others are open 7am–7pm.

Pay for fuel with cash – credit cards are not accepted (some banks issue special 'petrocards').
For expert advice contact the
Automobile Association of South Africa.
Tel: Toll free 0800 01 0101.

ELECTRICITY

Power is delivered at 220/230 volts AC, 50Hz. Sockets accept round, two-prong plugs. Adaptors are available at airports and stores in the cities and bigger towns.

EMBASSIES AND CONSULATES

South African consulates in selected countries are listed below. For further information, go the website of the **Department of Foreign Affairs.**
Tel: (012) 351 1000.
www.dfa.gov.za

Overseas

Australia

SA High Commission
Corner Rhodes Pl. and State Circle, Yarralumla, Canberra, ACT 2600.
Tel: (02) 62 73 2424.
www.rsa.emb.gov.au

Canada

South African Consulate
15 Sussex Drive, Ottawa, Ontario, K1M 1M8.
Tel: (613) 744 0330
www.rsafrica@southafrica-canada.com

Germany

South African Embassy
Tiergarten St 18, 10785 Berlin.
Tel: (30) 220 730.
www.suedafrika.org

United Kingdom

South African High Commission
South Africa House, Trafalgar Square. London WC2N5DP.
Tel: (207) 7451 7283.
info@saembassy.org

United States of America

Los Angeles:
South African Consulate
6300 Wilshire Boulevard, Suite 600, Los Angeles, CA 90048.
Tel (323) 651 0902.
sacgla@link2sa.com

New York:
South African Consulate General
333 East 38th St, New York, NY.
Tel: (212) 213 4880.

South Africa
Department of Home Affairs
Subdirectorate: Visas.
Private Bag X114, Pretoria 0001,
South Africa.
Tel. (012) 314 8911.
www.home-affairs.pwv.gov.za

EMERGENCIES
Police Emergency
Tel: 10111.

Ambulance, Fire, Mountain Rescue,
Poisoning, Air and Sea Rescue
Tel: 10177.

Child Emergency
Tel: 0800 123 321.
In case of difficulties with an emergency
call, Tel: 1022 and ask for the relevant
service.
The Thomas Cook Worldwide Customer
Promise offers free emergency assistance at
any Thomas Cook Network location to
travellers who have purchased their travel
tickets at a Thomas Cook Network
location.

GAY AND LESBIAN
Gay Net Cape Town
Details of the gay community in Cape
Town. Restaurants, clubs, events and so on.
Tel: (021) 422 1925.
www.gaynetcapetown.co.za

Gay and Lesbian Association of
Cape Town, Tourism, Industry and
Commerce
Website with extensive links to
accommodation entertainment and
other links.
www.galacttic.co.za

Most major car rental companies are represented
in Cape Town

Club Travel
Travel agency.
Tel: (021) 487 4218.
www.clubtravel.co.za

Africa Outing
Travel agency.
Tel: (021) 673 7377.
www.africaouting.com

GETTING AROUND
By Air
South African Airways, Kulala.com,
Nationwide and other airlines operate
domestic services between Cape Town
and major centres. They also fly to
selected smaller centres.

Several charter and safari operators fly to out-of-the-way places. Fixed wing aircraft and helicopters can be charted in all major centres. *(See also Arriving by Air on p174).*

By Rail

There is an efficient long-distance service connecting major cities. Trains also run to Botswana, Zimbabwe and Mozambique.

Some routes involve overnight travel – services include sleeping berths, private compartments and a dining car. First- and second-class tickets must be booked at least 24 hours in advance. When booking, ask about discounts and special offers.

Overnight trains have dining cars for first- and second-class travel. Cabins are comfortably fitted out with seats that are converted to bunks at night.

Shosholoza Main Line Services is run by **Spoornet**, the national rail system operator. Call central booking number in South Africa.
Tel: Toll free 086 000 8888.
International calls.
Tel: +27 11 773 8920.

Greyhound – a popular national bus service

By Bus and Coach

A large number of daily coach services operate on inter-city routes, day or night. Some services also run to Mozambique, Zimbabwe, Namibia and Botswana. Try to book your ticket 24 hours in advance.

Intercape

Reservations and enquiries.
Tel: (021) 380 4444.
www.intercape.co.za

Greyhound

Customer Care (Nationwide).
Tel: 083 915 9000 or
(011) 276 8500.
www.greyhound.co.za

Springbok-Atlas

Reservations and enquiries.
Tel: (021) 460 4700.
www.springbokatlas.com

Translux

One of the largest operators.
Reservations and enquiries.
Johannesburg: Tel: (011) 774 3333.
Cape Town: Tel: (021) 449 3333.
Durban: Tel: (031) 308 8111.
www.translux.co.za

The Baz Bus

Offers backpackers and budget travellers a service that takes in most of the major tourist attractions between Johannesburg, Durban and Cape Town including the Garden Route. Also to Swaziland. Flexible packages available.
Tel: (021) 439 2343.
www.bazbus.com

Hitch-hiking

Although hitch-hiking is widespread, as many South Africans do not own cars, it is inadvisable for tourists. Be cautious before giving lifts or accepting them.

HEALTH

AIDS

As everywhere, be cautious about HIV infection, and take the usual precautions. AIDS is highly prevalent in African countries, and South Africa is no exception. (*see Box, p18*)

Drinking Water

Tap water is purified and is 100 per cent safe to drink.

Hospitals and Doctors

Doctors are listed in local telephone directories under 'Medical Practitioners'. Most large hospitals have efficient casualty sections open 24 hours a day.

Inoculations

Visitors from most western countries do not require inoculation certificates. It is best, however, to seek medical advice if travelling through other parts of Africa before visiting South Africa.

Insects – Bites and Stings

In South Africa there are a number of insects or creatures that cause bites or stings. Most stings are relatively harmless and are soon forgotten, but some species of African bees, for example, are armed with quite virulent venom. Anti-histamine cream is usually adequate to ease the pain, but medical advice may be necessary, especially if there is an allergic reaction. When visiting game reserves or rural areas, it is a good idea to ensure children wear shoes at night as scorpions are often out and about hunting. Some have extremely toxic venom, and if someone gets stung, medical advice must be sought.

Blue bottles, which sometimes wash up on beaches, are small floating creatures that can deliver a painful sting. Life-guards usually offer assistance, but medical advice may be necessary.

Malaria and Bilharzia Precautions

Cape town is malaria-free because the *Anopheles* mosquitoes that carry the malaria parasite do not occur here. If you are travelling to Mpumalanga, Lowveld, Limpopo, the Kruger National Park and the game reserves of KwaZulu-Natal, you should take anti-malaria medication as prescribed by a doctor.

It is inadvisable to swim in some rivers and lakes in the eastern and northern regions of the country, as the bilharzia parasite may be present.

Sunburn

Skin cancer is one of the most common cancers among South Africans. Avoid the most intense hours of sunlight (11am–3pm), and remember that water provides little protection against ultraviolet (UV) radiation. Always wear a hat. Sun protection measures are essential for young children. Use sunscreen with at least an SPF 15+.

For more information on skin cancer, and the rules of sunbathing, call the **Cancer Association of South Africa.** *CANSA Tel: 0800 226 622.*

INSURANCE

Medical treatment must be paid for by the patient. It is wise to take out travel insurance which covers accidents, illness or hospitalisation. Travel insurance policies can be purchased through branches of Thomas Cook and most travel agents. Drivers' insurance can be taken out through car rental companies. **SA Tourmed** sells travellers' medical insurance that covers the entire southern Africa region.
Tel: (021) 979 4419.
www.sa-tourmed.com

MAPS

Excellent regional and city maps are available from South African Tourism and regional publicity associations nationwide. Most bookstores have a good range of local maps produced by Map Studio.

If you are travelling to the Kruger National Park, you should pick up the excellent maps and concise guides produced by Jacana Media.
Tel: (011) 648 1157.

MEDIA

The South African Broadcasting Corporation runs more than 18 radio stations broadcasting in 13 languages. It also broadcasts three major news and entertainment TV channels and one satellite channel. There are also a number of independent radio stations. Satellite TV with a large choice of international news and entertainment stations is widely available.

Thousands of periodicals, journals, newspapers and magazines are published on a regular basis. There are a number of national daily and Sunday papers –

Cape Times, The Argus, Die Burger, Rapport, Sunday Times, and *The Mail&Guardian.*

MONEY MATTERS
Currency

The South African currency unit is the rand, denoted by the symbol R (international symbol ZAR). It is divided into 100 cents (c). Bank notes are issued in denominations of R200, R100, R50, R20 and R10. Coins come in 1, 2, 5 (being phased out), 10, 20 and 50 cents; also Rl, R2 and R5 coins.

Exchange Facilities

Banks may request identification when changing money. Shop around for cheaper commission rates.

Money Transfers

If you need to transfer money quickly, go to any of the major banks for assistance.

Credit Cards

Most businesses, tour operators, air-lines, hotels and restaurants accept international credit cards including VISA, MasterCard, American Express and Diners Club. Petrol stations don't accept them.

A good place to start the week!

Currency is easily exchanged at Rennies Travel offices throughout South Africa (Thomas Cook's South African partner)

Thomas Cook

Thomas Cook traveller's cheques free you from the hazards of carrying large amounts of cash, and in the event of loss or theft, can quickly be refunded.

South African rand cheques are recommended, though cheques in all other currencies are acceptable. Many hotels, shops and restaurants in tourist and urban areas will accept traveller's cheques.

NATIONAL HOLIDAYS

1st January: New Year's Day.
21st March: Human Rights Day.
Variable: Good Friday.
Variable: Easter Monday.
27th April: Freedom Day.
1st May: Workers' Day.
16th June: Youth Day.
9th August: National Women's Day.
24th September: Heritage Day.
16th December: Day of Reconciliation.
25th December: Christmas Day.
26th December: Day of Goodwill.

OPENING HOURS
Banks
Open: Mon–Fri 9am–3.30pm, Sat 8.30–llam.

ATMs
ATMs are situated outside most banks, and are open 24 hours a day.

Shops
Shops are usually open Mon–Fri 8am–5pm, and Sat 8.30am–1pm. Some stores stay open all Sat & Sun.

Most major credit cards are accepted

PARKS AND RESERVES
South African National Parks

The Western Cape provincial government runs many of the smaller parks. Most parks in KwaZulu-Natal are run by Ezemvelo KZN Wildlife. The other provinces also run the smaller parks in their areas.

Entrances to parks and reserves close at sunset, but aim to arrive well before that.

It is best to do thorough research before booking accommodation to ensure that your wildlife experience meets your expectations. Travel agents will be willing to help, or visit the following websites.

South African National Parks
www.park-sa.co.za
Cape Nature Conservation
www.capenature.org
KZN Wildlife
www.kznwildlife.com
South Africa Tourism
www.southafrica.net
Call centre: 083 123 2345.

Smaller Parks and Private Reserves
Regional tourism offices will have details of smaller parks (*see Regional Tourism Websites on p188*). Most travel agents and the South African Tourism website have details of private game reserves and lodges.

PHARMACIES

There are numerous pharmacies nationwide, and they are easy to find. Should you require medicine after hours, it is best to ask at the hotel or B&B, as very few pharmacies stay open at night. Some private hospitals have pharmacies that are sometimes open later than others.

PLACES OF WORSHIP

Churches of every denomination, synagogues, mosques and Hindu temples are all represented in abundance.

Generally, South Africa's population is religiously oriented, and religious beliefs play an important role in public affairs.

LANGUAGE

USEFUL TRANSLATED PHRASES

English: Yes
Afrikaans: Ja
Xhosa: Ewe

English: No
Afrikaans: Nee
Xhosa: Hayi

English: How are you?
Afrikaans: Hoe gaan dit?
Xhosa: Kunjani?

English: Thank you
Afrikaans: Dankie
Xhosa: Enkosi

English: How much?
Afrikaans: Hoeveel?
Xhosa: Yimalini?

English: Good morning
Afrikaans: Goeiemore
Xhosa: Molo

English: Where is the post office/bank/hotel?
Afrikaans: Waar is die poskantoor/bank/hotel?
Xhosa: Iphi iposi/ibhanki/ihotele?

POLICE

The South African Police Service (SAPS) can be contacted 24 hours a day. See listings as SA Police Service under Government Departments in local phone directories.

Many small hotels and B&Bs may also hire the services of private security companies that respond to burglar alarms. Management will give you details if applicable.

POST OFFICE

Post office hours are Mon–Fri 8.30am–4.30pm, Sat 9am–12pm. Letters and parcels can also be mailed via the Post Net chain of stores that has branches nationwide.

PRICES AND TAX

South African prices have increased considerably over the past few years, so it is worth doing some research before booking accommodation and tours.

Having said that, petrol is relatively inexpensive, as are local wines and spirits.

VAT, currently at the rate of 14 per cent, is levied on most items and services, including hotel accommodation, goods, transport and tours. You can claim VAT back on goods priced higher than R250. The original tax invoice, the VAT refund control sheet, your passport, and the item are required. Please refer to the VAT shop at the international airport of departure to claim the VAT back.

PUBLIC TRANSPORT

Public transport in most South African cities is erratic. There are bus services in most of the bigger cities, but they tend to stick to limited routes, run infrequently and close down at night.

Mini bus taxis are the most common form of public transport, but the standard of driving is usually poor and the vehicles are often uncomfortable and sometimes un-roadworthy.

Cape Town has a reasonably efficient suburban and city rail service.

Taxis can be arranged by hotels, restaurants or by looking in the Yellow Pages telephone directory. Ask for a quote before setting off.

SENIOR CITIZENS

Facilities for senior citizens are not comprehensive. In general, expect discounts on cinema, theatre tickets and some museums. If you feel you should be offered a pensioners' discount, it's best to ask.

St Mary's Catholic Church, Cape Town

**The Association for Retired Persons
and Pensioners**
Tel: (021) 531 1768.
Age in Action
Tel: (021) 426 4249.

STUDENT AND YOUTH TRAVEL

Hostelling International South Africa
(HISA) helps provide student cards,
information about discounts and other
services.
73 St Georges Mall, 3rd Floor, George House.
Tel: (021) 442 2251.
www.hisa.org.za

TELEPHONES

South African telephone call charges
are expensive, and hotels add a significant
charge to your call. Phone cards for
public phones can be purchased in
supermarkets, at post offices and so on.
Other public telephones accept coins.

The international dialling code for
South Africa is 27. Cell phones (mobile
phones) can be rented at airports and at
cell phone stores. Most UK cell phones
will work in South Africa. The country
has an extensive cell phone network, and
renting a cell phone is a far more reliable
way of communicating than relying on
public telephones.

Dialling codes

The dialling codes for the main cities
within South Africa are:
Cape Town: 021.
Durban: 031.
Johannesburg: 011.
Pretoria: 012.

Useful numbers

Directory Enquiries: 1023.

International Operator
For booking or placing international
calls: 0900.
International Directory Enquiries:
0903.

THOMAS COOK

The Thomas Cook Network partner in
South Africa is Rennies Travel, with
branches throughout the country.
Rennies offer foreign exchange,
commission-free cashing of traveller's
cheques and other services.
Rennies Travel Foreign Exchange
24 hours, nationwide.
Tel: toll free 0861 11 11 77.

TIME

South African Standard Time throughout
the year is two hours ahead of Greenwich
Mean Time (Universal Standard Time),
one hour ahead of Central European
Winter Time, seven hours ahead of US
Eastern Standard Winter Time and eight
hours behind Australian Eastern
Standard Time.

TIPPING

A 10 per cent service charge is generally
expected in restaurants, not usually
included with the bill. Raise the tip to
15 per cent if you have been particularly
well treated. Leave something for
hotel staff such as porters and
chambermaids.

Taxi drivers should receive 5 per cent
of the fare on top, and luggage porters
R5 per bag.

TOILETS

Most tourist venues, service stations
and shopping centres are fairly well

South Africa has a good, well maintained network

served by public lavatories. In nature reserves and national parks, standards of cleanliness are usually fairly high.

TOURIST OFFICES
South Africa Tourism
Bonjala House, 90 Protea Rd, Chiselhurston, Sandton.
Tel: (011) 895 3000.
www.southafrica.net

Australia
South African Tourism
Level 1, 117 York St, Sydney, NSW 2000.
PO Box Q120, QVB NSW 1230.
Tel: +61 2 9261 5000.
Fax: +61 2 9261 2000.
blanche@southafricantourism.com.au

France
South African Tourism
61 Rue La Boetie, 75008 Paris.
Tel: +33 1 456 10197.
Fax: +33 1 456 10196.
satourism@afriquedusud-tourisme.fr

Germany
South African Tourism
Friedensstr. 6-10, Frankfurt, 60311.
Tel: +49 69 92 91 290.
Fax: +49 69 28 0950.
info@southafricantourism.de

Italy
South African Tourism
Via Mascheroni, 19 – 5 Floor, 20145, Milano.
Tel: +39 02 4391 1765.
Fax: +39 02 4391 1158.
info@turismosudafricano.com

United Kingdom
South African Tourism
6 Alt Grove, London, SW19 4DZ, United Kingdom.
PO Box 49110, Wimbledon, SW19 4XZ.
Tel: + 44 (0) 20 8971 9364.
Fax: + 44 (0) 20 8944 6705.
info@uk.southafrica.net

United States of America
South African Tourism
500 5th Ave, 20th Floor, Suite 2040, New York NY 10110.
Tel: +91 212 730 2929.
Fax: +91 212 764 1980.
newyork@southafrica.net

Regional Tourism Offices in South Africa
Eastern Cape Tourism
Tel: (0431) 701 9600.
www.etourism.co.za

Free State Tourism
Tel: (051) 430 8206.
www.fstourism.co.za

Gauteng Tourism
Tel: (011) 327 2000.
www.gauteng.net

KwaZulu-Natal Tourism
Tel: (031) 366 7500.
www.kzn.org

Limpopo Tourism
Tel: (015) 295 8262.
www.limpopotourism.org

Mpumalanga Tourism
Tel: (013) 752 7001.
www.mpumalanga.com

Northern Cape Tourism
Tel: (053) 832 2697.
www.northerncape.org.za

North West Tourism
Tel: (018) 386 1225.
www.tourismnorthwest.co.za

Western Cape Tourism
Tel: (021) 426 4260.
www.capetourism.org

TRAVELLERS WITH DISABILITIES

For information about special-needs tours accommodating wheelchairs, services, handbooks and so on, contact the following organisations.
National Council for the Physically Disabled in South Africa
Tel: (011) 726 8040.

South African National Council – Blind
Tel: (012) 346 1171.

South African National Council – Deaf
Tel: (011) 482 1610.

Conversion Table		
FROM	TO	MULTIPLY BY
Inches	Centimetres	2.54
Feet	Metres	0.3048
Yards	Metres	0.9144
Miles	Kilometres	1.6090
Acres	Hectares	0.4047
Gallons	Litres	4.5460
Ounces	Grams	28.35
Pounds	Grams	453.6
Pounds	Kilograms	0.4536
Tons	Tonnes	1.0160

To convert back, for example from centimetres to inches, divide by the number in the third column.

Men's Suits

SA/UK	36	38	40	42	44	46	48
Rest of Europe	46	48	50	52	54	56	58
USA	36	38	40	42	44	46	48

Dress Sizes

SA/UK		8	10	12	14	16	18
France		36	38	40	42	44	46
Italy		38	40	42	44	46	48
Rest of Europe		34	36	38	40	42	44
USA		6	8	10	12	14	16

Men's Shirts

SA/UK	14	14.5	15	15.5	16	16.5	17
Rest of Europe	36	37	38	39/40	41	42	43
USA	14	14.5	15	15.5	16	16.5	17

Men's Shoes

SA/UK		7	7.5	8.5	9.5	10.5	11
Rest of Europe	41		42	43	44	45	46
USA		8	8.5	9.5	10.5	11.5	12

Women's Shoes

SA/UK		4.5	5	5.5	6	6.5	7
Rest of Europe	38		38	39	39	40	41
USA		6	6.5	7	7.5	8	8.5

A trail for the blind in Kirstenbosch Gardens

Caring for Places we Visit

The Travel Foundation is a UK charity that cares for places we love to visit. You can help us protect the natural environment, traditions and culture – the things that make your visit special. And improve the well-being of local families – spreading the benefit of your visit to those who most need it. All of which can make your holiday experience even better! Most importantly, you can help ensure that there are great places for us all to visit – for generations to come.

What you can do:

- Remove any packaging from items before you go on holiday and recycle if possible.
- Do hire local guides and book locally-run excursions – it will enrich your holiday experience and help support local families.
- Hire a car only if you need to. Using public transport, bicycles and walking are 'environmentally-friendlier' alternatives.
- Respect local culture and traditions. Ensure your dress and behaviour is appropriate for the places you visit. Ask permission before taking photographs of people or their homes.
- Turn down/off heating or air conditioning when not required. Switch off lights and turn the television off rather than leave on standby.

- Do use water sparingly. Take showers instead of baths, and inform staff if you are happy to re-use towels and bed linen rather than replace daily.
- Don't pick flowers and plants or collect pebbles, seashells, coral or starfish. Leave them for others to enjoy.
- Don't buy products made from endangered plants or animals, including hardwoods, ivory, corals, reptiles or turtles. If in doubt – don't buy.
- Do buy locally-made products – shopping in locally-owned outlets and treating yourself to local food and drink is a great way to get into the holiday spirit and also benefits local families.
- Always bargain with humour, and bear in mind that a small cash saving to you could be a significant amount to the seller.
- Coral is extremely fragile. Don't step on it or remove it, and avoid kicking up sand.

For more tips and information on The Travel Foundation and its work, please visit *www.thetravelfoundation.org.uk*.

**the
travel foundation**
caring for places we love to visit

ACKNOWLEDGEMENTS

Thomas Cook Publishing wishes to thank the following photographers for the photographs reproduced in this book, to whom the copyright in the photographs belong:

Mike Cadman: 7, 13, 14, 18–22, 24, 44, 48, 49, 53, 60, 64, 66, 68, 71, 81, 84, 98, 102–106, 116, 122, 124, 126–128, 131, 133, 142, 143, 146, 147, 154, 155, 160, 162, 164, 165, 168, 173, 174, 180, 182, 183, 187

Trevor Samson: Contents page, 4, 5, 6, 10–12, 15–17, 23, 26, 27, 30–34, 36–43, 45–47, 50, 51, 52, 54–59, 59, 61–65, 69–71, 74, 76, 78–80, 82–89, 92, 93, 95–98, 100, 106, 107, 110, 112–116, 119, 120, 123, 142, 144, 145, 148–153, 156, 160, 163, 166, 167, 173, 175, 179, 185

All remaining pictures have been credited on the relevant pages.